C000263423

Collins

AQA GCSE 9-1
English Language
& Literature

Workbook

Paul Burns

Contents

Contents

Poetry

Practice Exam Papers

Key Technical Skills: Writing

Spelling

1 Put the following words into their plural forms:

a) tomato ___*tomatoes*___   b) birthday ___*birthdays*___

c) soliloquy ___*soliloquies*___   d) family ___*families*___

e) parenthesis ___*parentheses*___   **[5]**

2 Insert the correctly spelled word in each of the following pairs of sentences:

a) **Your/you're**

___*you're*___ not going out like that.

I asked ___*your*___ sister to bring it.

b) **There/they're/their**

___*there*___ are twenty-five people in the class.

They have all done ___*their*___ homework but ___*they're*___ not sitting in the right places.

c) **Where/wear/we're**

Turn it off or it will ___*wear*___ out.

We have no idea ___*where*___ it is but ~~*we're*~~ going anyway.

d) **Past/passed**

I ___*passed*___ him in the street an hour ago.

He walked right ___*past*___ me as if I wasn't there.

e) **To/too/two**

There were only ___*two*___ exams ___*to*___ sit but that was one ___*too*___ many.

f) **Practice/practise**

If you don't go to the ___*practice*___ you'll be left out of the team.

If you want to improve you will have to ___*practise*___ every day.   **[15]**

3 The following passage includes ten incorrect spellings. Find them and circle them, then write the correct spellings below.

> Last (nite) I went to the cinema with my friend Bob and his (farther) Michael. The whole evening was not very (succesfull). The cinema was very (crouded) and we had to sit (seperately). Then, it turned out the film was in a (forrein) (langauge) and (no-one) could understand it. I think it was about the (enviroment). Afterwards, Michael took us to a (resturant) were we had pizzas.

___*night*___   ___*successful*___   ___*father*___   ___*foreign*___

___*environment*___   ___*restaurant*___   ~~*cow*~~ ___*crowded*___

___*language*___   ___*separately*___   ___*no one*___   **[10]**

Total Marks _____ **/ 30**

Key Technical Skills: Writing

1 Punctuate the following passage using only commas and full stops. There should be a total of five punctuation marks.

> *Great Expectations,* one of the best-known novels by Charles Dickens, is the story of Pip, a boy who grows up in the marshes of Kent. At the beginning of the story, he meets an escaped convict in the churchyard where his parents are buried.

[5]

2 Add ten apostrophes, where necessary, to the following passage:

> At about ten o'clock, we went to Romio's for pizzas. I'm not sure what Bob's pizza topping was but I had ham and pineapple. I wish I hadn't because later on I was sick in Michael's car. It's brand new and I thought he'd be angry but he wasn't. We're not going there again.

[10]

3 Add a question mark, an exclamation mark, a colon, a semi-colon or parentheses (brackets) to the following clauses so that they make sense:

a)	Who was that masked man? nobody knows.	
b)	The cat slept quietly on the mat; the dog slept noisily on the step.	
c)	I don't believe it! that's the first answer I've got.	
d)	Annie deserved the prize: she was the best baker by far.	
e)	Jane and Elizabeth (the two oldest Bennet sisters) get married at the end.	

[5]

Key Technical Skills: Writing

1 Identify whether the sentences below are simple, compound, complex or minor sentences:

   a) I confess that I had my doubts when I reflected upon the great traffic which had passed along the London road in the interval. _____

   b) Very clearly. _____

   c) We all need help sometimes. _____

   d) Mr Collins was punctual to his time, and was received with great politeness by the whole family. _____

   e) Elizabeth smiled. _____   **[5]**

2 Combine the following sentences to form complex sentences, using the conjunctions **because**, **although** or **until**.

   a) I bought Anna a bunch of flowers. It was her birthday.

     _____

     _____

   b) He did not finish the race. They gave him a certificate.

     _____

     _____

   c) I kept going. I reached the finishing line.

     _____

     _____   **[3]**

3 Use the following sentences to form a complex sentence using a relative pronoun:

Joey was the oldest cat in the street. He never left the garden.

_____

_____

_____   **[1]**

4 Use the following sentences to form a complex sentence without using a connective:

I was walking down the street. I realized I had forgotten my phone.

_____

_____

_____   **[1]**

Total Marks _____ **/ 10**

Key Technical Skills: Writing

Text Structure and Organization

1 Rearrange the following paragraphs so that the passage makes sense. Write the paragraphs in the correct order below.

a) As a result of this, the student body has decided to appeal to the governors. Jodie has written a letter to every governor, setting out the problems as the students see them.

b) As yet no replies have been received. The increasingly angry students are starting to consider taking 'direct action'.

c) Jodie Collins, a spokesperson for the students, has had several meetings about the issue with the Principal. Ms Rundle apparently listened to the students' points, but later sent an email claiming that nothing can be done because of lack of funds.

d) According to this letter, students' health and safety are at risk. Among other things, toilets are not properly cleaned and standards of hygiene in the kitchen leave a lot to be desired.

e) Students of Summerfield College have expressed concern about the environment they have to work in. They have a number of complaints.

....

....

....

....

....

....

....

....

....

....

[5]

2 Insert each of these five discourse markers or connectives into the passage so that it makes sense:

nevertheless   when   subsequently   in spite of   however

(a) .... I read your letter I was shocked by its contents. **(b)** ....
being a governor of the college, I was completely unaware of the issues which you mention.
I have **(c)** .... been in touch with Ms Rundle to express my concern. She
(d), ..., has not responded to my letters. **(e)** ...., I shall
continue to press her for answers.   [5]

Total Marks .... / 10

Key Technical Skills: Writing

Standard English and Grammar

1 Insert the correct form of the verb 'to be' or 'to do':

Present tense

a) You _____ a great singer.

b) They _____ trying hard.

Simple past

c) We _____ waiting for you.

d) He _____ what they told him to do.

Perfect

e) She _____ my friend for years.

f) They _____ all their exams now.

Simple past + past perfect

g) We _____ happy because we _____ all the exercises. **[7]**

2 Which of the following is correct in Standard UK English? Circle the correct word.

a) The defendant **pleaded/pled** guilty.

b) He's one of the **only/few** people who can do that.

c) He has **got/gotten** two coffees. **[3]**

3 Change the following dialogue to Standard English:

Jo: Hey. How are you guys doing?

Arthur: Good. Real good.

Jo: Wanna drink?

Arthur: Can I get two coffees?

Jo: Sure. Where are you sat?

_____

_____

_____

_____ **[5]**

4 Rewrite the following passage in Standard English:

> I was stood in the street when Frankie come over. I give him a smile and opened me gob to speak. I was gonna ask him how he done in math. I never said nothing. Soon as I seen him I knew he done good.

_____

_____

_____

_____ **[5]**

Key Technical Skills: Reading

1 Read the passage below:

> The tower of St Peter's church was, until very recently, the tallest building in the town. On a clear day, it can still be seen from miles away. However, it is now overshadowed by a brutal example of modern architecture. Built two years ago, and twice as high as the church tower, the Kingsley Tower dominates the surrounding landscape.

Look at the statements below. Which of them are explicitly stated in the text? Tick the correct answers.

a) The church tower used to be the tallest building in town. ☐

b) Everyone hates the new building. ☐

c) The Kingsley Tower is taller than the church tower. ☐

d) The writer does not like modern architecture. ☐ **[2]**

2 Read the passage below:

List four things that we learn about the old gentleman's appearance.

> It was by the Green Dragon that the old gentleman travelled. He was a very nice looking old gentleman, and he looked as if he were nice, too, which is not at all the same thing. He had a fresh-coloured, clean-shaven face, and white hair, and he wore rather odd-shaped collars and a top hat that wasn't exactly the same kind as other people's. Of course the children didn't see all this at first. In fact, the first thing they noticed about the old gentleman was his hand.
>
> From *The Railway Children* by E. Nesbit

....

....

....

....

....

....

....

.... **[4]**

Total Marks	/ 6

Key Technical Skills: Reading

Implicit Information and Ideas

1 True or false?

Read the passage below and tick four statements below which are TRUE.

> Work experience is an established part of today's school calendar. All Year 10 pupils in all schools have to do it. But why? I decided to ask around and found the general opinion amongst the adults I asked was that it would prepare young people for the world of work. I have to say, though, that none of them sounded terribly convinced and I got the distinct impression that they were just following the party line.
>
> Assuming the object of the exercise is to prepare us for the world of work, does it? My placement was in my uncle's office. He is a solicitor and the rationale behind the placement was that I had expressed an interest in studying Law. That sounds logical. But what did I learn? I learned that you should dress smartly and be punctual. I learned how to answer the telephone politely. I learned that solicitors drink an awful lot of coffee. I could have found out all of that just by having a chat with my uncle.

a) Work experience is compulsory in Year 10. ☐

b) Most adults are against work experience. ☐

c) The writer thinks the adults did not give their true opinions. ☐

d) The writer questions the value of work experience. ☐

e) The writer does not want to be a solicitor. ☐

f) The writer found work experience challenging and stimulating. ☐

g) It is important to turn up to work on time. ☐

h) The writer thinks work experience is important. ☐

[4]

Key Technical Skills: Reading

Summary

1 Reduce each of the following sentences to five words to give the necessary information without losing sense.

a) Stunning trees stand like soldiers behind the shed.	
b) Charlotte Green, the girl with blonde hair, ate Lydia's chocolate.	
c) I demand that you tell me now who did it.	

[3]

2 Read this statement from the witness to a crime.

> I was walking down our street – Arbuckle Lane – at nine o'clock on Monday. I know it was nine o'clock because I was worried about being late for work and I looked at my watch. As I passed number eighteen, the big house with the yellow front door where Mrs Lightbody used to live, I heard a noise, so I stopped and turned around. There were two men on the step and one of them had something in his hand, which he was using to break the glass in the door. I shouted out and they turned. One of them was tall, about six foot, with a grey beard – he reminded me of someone on the television – and the other one was stocky with curly black hair. When they saw me the tall man dropped something and they both ran. It gave me quite a turn.

If you were investigating the crime, which FIVE of the following pieces of information would be relevant to solving it? Tick the correct answers.

a) Mrs Lightbody lived at number eighteen. ☐

b) One of the men was six foot tall. ☐

c) He used something to break the glass in the door. ☐

d) The witness was worried about being late. ☐

e) The witness lives in Arbuckle Lane. ☐

f) The tall man dropped something. ☐

g) One man had curly black hair. ☐

h) It was nine o'clock. ☐   [5]

3 On a separate piece of paper, write a summary of the statement. Aim for 70 words or fewer. [12]

Total Marks _____ / 20

Key Technical Skills: Reading

1 Read the two passages below.

Pick out as many differences as you can between the two girls' experiences of school and write them in the table below or on a separate piece of paper.

> **Mary Jane:** I grew up on a farm near Barrow. My parents were not at all happy about me going to school, but they were told it was the law and I had to go. They couldn't see the point of it. But I loved school and I never missed a day. The school was a low stone building in the centre of the village. There were two huge rooms, one for the juniors and one for the infants. There were forty pupils in my class and we sat in rows, facing the teacher. We worked really hard all day, except for playtime, and we were not allowed to speak at all unless spoken to. Miss Murdishaw was very strict. We did like her, though, and she only gave you the cane if you were very naughty.
>
> **Sarah:** I would never have gone to school at all if I'd had my way. But I was never allowed to stay off. 'Education, education, education', my mum used to say, 'that's what you need in life. Miss a day's school and you'll regret it'. My first school was in the village near where we lived. There were twenty-four children in our class and we used to sit around tables in groups of six. All my group did was talk, talk, talk all day long. I don't think we did much work at all. The teacher just wandered around the room smiling at us and telling us everything we did was brilliant. She never punished anyone really, not even telling them off. I think she thought we all loved her, but I certainly didn't.

Mary Jane	Sarah

[10]

2 Now sum up the differences between the girls' experiences of school, writing in proper sentences.

....

....

....

....

....

....

[8]

Total Marks .... / 18

Referring to the Text

1 Match each statement (**a–c**) with its paraphrase (**d–f**):

a) The modern apartments are situated close to all amenities. ✓

b) Six o'clock struck on the bells of the church that was so conveniently near to the solicitor's dwelling, and still he was digging at the problem. ✗

c) She suggested liaising outside the church at 18.05. I said yes. ✗

d) The lawyer was still trying to work it out in the evening. ✗

e) The flats are up-to-date and near shops and transport. ✓

f) We agreed to meet at about six o'clock by the church. ✗

[3]

2 The following sentences all include quotations from *Macbeth* which have not been set out correctly. Set them out correctly, using colons and/or quotation marks where appropriate.

a)	Macbeth refers to the prophecies as happy prologues.	Macbeth refers to the prophecies as 'happy prologues'.	✓
b)	He tells us that one of them has come true I am Thane of Cawdor.	He tells us that one of them has come true: 'I am Thane of Cawdor'	✓
c)	Macbeth asks how the prophecies can be evil when the witches have told the truth If ill, Why hath it given me earnest of success Commencing in a truth?	Macbeth ~~tells~~ asks how the prophecies can be evil: when the witches have told the truth if ill, 'Why hath it given me earnest of success Commencing in a truth?'.	✗

[6]

3 The following sentences are an example of the use of PEE. Identify the point, the evidence and the explanation.

Frankenstein's response is negative from the start. Referring to the experiment as a 'catastrophe' and his creation as a 'wretch' suggests that he has rejected the creature and will not try to find any good in it.

Point	Frankensteins response is negative from the start ✓
Evidence	Refers to experiment as a 'catastrophe' and his creation a 'wretch' ✓
Explanation	Suggest rejection and dislike of the creature ✓

[3]

Total Marks 8 / 12

Key Technical Skills: Reading

Analysing Language 1

1 How would you describe the register of the following sentences?

Choose from:

formal

technical

dialectical

colloquial

a) 'Appen he were took badly but he'll be all reet. ....

b) It may be that the gentleman was feeling ill. It is, however, likely that he will recover.

....

c) Me mate wasn't feeling too good but he's OK now. ....

d) The patient suffered a brief episode of disequilibrium, which could be a symptom of a number of chronic conditions.

....   [4]

2 Read the passage below and identify the word class (part of speech) of the highlighted words:

> Since the party, she had been more **eager** than ever, and had planned many ways of making friends **with** him; **but** he had not been seen lately, and Jo began to think he had gone away, when she one day spied a brown face at an upper **window**, looking **wistfully** down into their garden, where Beth and Amy **were snowballing** one another.
>
> From *Little Women* by Louisa May Alcott

a) eager		b) with	
c) but		d) window	
e) wistfully		f) were snowballing	

[6]

3 a) The passage above is only one sentence. What sort of sentence is it? ....

b) Give an example from the passage of a proper noun. ....

c) Is the clause 'he had not been seen lately' in the active or passive voice? ....

d) What tense is 'had planned' in the first line? ....

e) In what 'person' is the narrative written? ....   [5]

Key Technical Skills: Reading

Analysing Language 2

1 State whether each of the following sentences contains a metaphor or a simile and describe the effect of the comparison.

	Metaphor or simile?	What is its effect?
a) He ran like the wind.		
b) An army of insects invaded the kitchen.		
c) Her heart was as cold as ice.		

[6]

2 Read the passage below. Find an example of each of the techniques listed in the table below.

> Time was not on their side. The fire fizzed and crackled around them as the brave Brown brothers entered the building. Inside, great flames came in waves.

a) personification	
b) onomatopoeia	

[2]

3 Read the passage below, from *The Hound of the Baskervilles* by Arthur Conan Doyle.

> October 16th – A dull and foggy day, with a drizzle of rain. The house is banked with rolling clouds, which rise now and then to show the dreary curves of the moor, with thin, silver veins upon the sides of the hills, and the distant boulders gleaming where the light strikes upon their wet faces. It is melancholy outside and in. The baronet is in a black reaction after the excitements of the night. I am conscious myself of a weight at my heart and a feeling of impending danger – ever-present, which is the more terrible because I am unable to define it.
>
> And have I not cause for such a feeling?

How does the writer use language to describe the thoughts and feelings of the narrator?

On a separate piece of paper, comment on:

- the writer's choice of words and phrases
- language features and techniques
- sentence form.

[8]

Total Marks _____ / 16

Key Technical Skills: Reading

Analysing Form and Structure

1 Here is the opening of a short story (*The Count and the Wedding Guest* by O. Henry).

> One evening when Andy Donovan went to dinner at his Second Avenue boarding-house, Mrs Scott introduced him to a new boarder, a young lady, Miss Conway. Miss Conway was small and unobtrusive. She wore a plain, snuffy-brown dress, and bestowed her interest, which seemed languid, upon her plate. She lifted her diffident eyelids and shot one perspicuous, judicial glance at Mr Donovan, politely murmured his name, and returned to her mutton. Mr Donovan bowed with the grace and beaming smile that were rapidly winning for him social, business and political advancement, and erased the snuffy-brown one from the tablets of his consideration.

a) What do we learn about the story's setting?

   It is set at boarding houses and it is the evening [2]

b) What is your first impression of Miss Conway?

   She is ~~so~~ shy ~~and friendly~~ and polite. [2]

c) What is the effect of the phrase 'shot one perspicuous, judicial glance'?

   She is a bit Judgemental. [2]

d) What does the description of Andy Donovan's response tell us about him?

   He is a gentleman that is kind and friendly [2]

e) What do you think might happen next?

   Mr Donovan and Miss Conway will talk about something [2]

2 Match the endings **a–c** with the descriptions **x–z**.

a)	Honour the charge they made! Honour the Light Brigade, Noble six hundred!	x)	This ending draws a lesson from the story.
b)	...the wishes, the hopes, the confidence, the predictions of the small band of true friends who witnessed the ceremony, were fully answered in the perfect happiness of the union.	y)	This ending might inspire the reader.
c)	'Was I not right?' said the little Mouse. Little friends may prove great friends.	z)	A happy ending, leaving the reader satisfied.

[3]

Total Marks _____ / 13

English Language 1

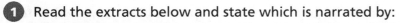

Creative Reading 1

1 Read the extracts below and state which is narrated by:

A naive/unreliable narrator	
An omniscient narrator	
A reliable first-person narrator	
An intrusive narrator	

[8]

> **A**   She told me to pray every day, and whatever I asked for I would get it. But it warn't so. I tried it. Once I got a fish-line but no hooks. It warn't any good to me without hooks. I tried for hooks three or four times, but somehow I couldn't make it work.
>
> From *The Adventures of Huckleberry Finn* by Mark Twain

> **B**   The extract from my private diary which forms the last chapter has brought my narrative up to the 18th of October, a time when these strange events began to move swiftly towards their terrible conclusion.
>
> From *The Hound of the Baskervilles* by Sir Arthur Conan Doyle

> **C**   As John Bold will occupy much of our attention, we must endeavour to explain who he is, and why he takes the part of John Hiram's beadsmen.
>
> From *The Warden* by Anthony Trollope

> **D**   Mr James Duffy lived in Chapelizod because he wished to live as far as possible from the city of which he was a citizen and because he found all the other suburbs of Dublin mean, modern and pretentious.
>
> From *Dubliners* by James Joyce

Total Marks .... / 8

Creative Reading 2

1 Look at the quotations in the table. In the third column (or on a separate piece of paper) enter how we learn about character, choosing from:

a) Narrator's description

b) What the character says

c) What others say about/to the character

d) What the character does

e) How others react to the character

In the fourth column (or on a separate piece of paper) say what we learn about the character.

Character	Quotation	How we learn about the character	What we learn
Hyde's housekeeper *The Strange Case of Dr Jekyll and Mr Hyde*	She had an evil face, smoothed by hypocrisy; but her manners were excellent.	A	Not sincere good mannered
Magwitch *Great Expectations*	'Hold your noise!' cried a terrible voice […] 'Keep still, you little devil, or I'll cut your throat.'	B	Shouty ~~Keep stil~~ Horrid
Darcy *Pride and Prejudice*	[Darcy] was looked at with great admiration for about half the evening, till his manners gave a disgust which turned the tide of his popularity.	D/E	Good mannered till annoyed Popular before manner change
Mrs Reed *Jane Eyre*	Mrs Reed, impatient of my now frantic anguish and wild sobs, abruptly thrust me back and locked me in…	~~~~ D/A	Impatient ~~~~ Possibly angry
Victor Frankenstein *Frankenstein*	'My dear Victor,' cried he, 'what, for God's sake, is the matter? Do not laugh in that manner. How ill you are!'	C	Concerned Very Questioning

[15]

Total Marks _____ / 15

English Language 1

Narrative Writing

Imagine you have been set the following task:

'Write a story about someone who wins a huge amount of money in the lottery.'

Use the following questions and points to help you create a plan for your writing.

1 Character and Voice

a) What person will you write in? If first person, is the narrator also the protagonist?

First person

b) What kind of register will the narrator use?

~~It's a normal story~~ a bit comical, but mostly like a normal story

c) On a separate piece of paper, make notes on your protagonist's:

- gender – *man*
- age – *17-18*
- appearance – *~~Brown hair, blue eyes~~ Casual, healthy, smart*
- background – *Well off, rather rich*
- relationships – *group of friends to, lives with 2 parents,*
- way of speaking – *Uses some Slang but mostly normal speach* [8]

2 Place and Time

a) Where does it start?

At home

b) Does the setting change during the story?

yes

c) When is it set – now, in the past or in the future?

Present

d) How long does the story take?

Day in the life of the character

e) Will it be written in chronological order?

Yes [5]

3 Structure

On a separate piece of paper, make notes on your:

- exposition – *~~Wakes up~~ has a boring morning*
- inciting incident – *Goes ~~to the pub~~ with friends,*
- turning point(s) – *taking part in a competition between his friends*
- climax – *Winning*
- coda (ending) – *goes home in glee* [5]

Total Marks ____ / 18

English Language 1

Descriptive Writing

Choose one of the following tasks and answer the questions below:

Either

Describe someone who lives in your street.

Or

Describe a visit to a fairground.

Use the following questions and points to help you create a plan for your writing.

1 **a)** Are you going to use the first or third person? _____

      b) Are you going to use the past or present tense? _____ [2]

2 Using an adjective and a noun for each, jot down at least two things you can:

      a) see _____

      b) hear _____

      c) smell _____

      d) taste _____

      e) touch _____ [10]

3 Make notes on the scene/person from:

      a) long distance _____

_____

_____

      b) middle distance _____

_____

_____

      c) close up _____

_____

_____ [6]

4 Imagery

Write down an appropriate:

      a) simile _____

_____

      b) metaphor _____

_____ [2]

Total Marks _____ / 20

English Language 2

Reading Non-fiction 1 and 2

1. Read the following short texts and use the table below to list differences in the writers' points of view and how they are expressed.

A

It's easy to miss Little Mickledon. It's a tiny village, with no shop or pub, nestling in a valley surrounded by fields of grazing sheep. It's a bit like stepping back in time to the Olde England of yore. It's charming and tranquil, cut off from 'civilization' by having no broadband and no mobile phone signal. But for visitors to Alf and Maisie's delightful bed and breakfast, that's a big attraction. 'People come here to relax', beams Maisie, 'and to rediscover a sense of inner peace and calm.'

B

The Bideaway B & B, Little Mickledon, was a massive disappointment. We were promised peace and quiet, sure, but we didn't expect to be totally cut off from the modern world. Be warned. There's no broadband and we couldn't get a mobile signal. When we complained – not our only complaint: the rooms were grubby and the breakfast pitiful – the hippy owners just shrugged their shoulders.

	Text A	Text B
What is the writer's attitude to Little Mickledon?	It is a nice place to be with a beautiful landscape	The writer hated it there. 'massive' 'we didn't expect to be cut off from the modern world.'
What is the writer's opinion of the B & B?	A great place to go and relax and a "has 'delightful bed and breakfast"	They described it as 'grubby' and 'a massive disappointment'
What impression do you get of the writer?	My impression of the writer is they make the most of anything and everything	My impression of the writer is that they expect more and doesn't like the lack of internet.
How would you describe the general tone and style?	This extract has an optimistic happy tone and is styled to advertise the village and B&B	This extract has a very negative tone and is styled as a warning rather than a review
Comment on language features.	'Nestling in a valley' the use of personification gives the sense that the valley is the villages home and where it belongs.	'Be warned' the use of an imperative shows how disappointed the writer was and how you would be as well.

[20]

Total Marks _____ / 20

English Language 2

1 Imagine you have been asked to give your opinion on the statement 'Work Experience is a complete waste of time and should be abolished'.

Use the table below to list five arguments in favour of abolishing work experience (pro) and five against it (con).

Pros	Cons
Gives you first hand experiance of the real world.	Can be boring it you pick the wrong one to do.
Helps develop and get you ready for a future job.	
Allows you to see how the Job is done.	
Can make you change carrier path by gaining new interests in a job	

[10]

2 The statement above was made in an article in your local newspaper. Decide whether you agree or disagree with it and write only **the opening paragraph** of a letter to the newspaper expressing your view.

I am writing to show ~~how~~ the extent to which I strongly disagree with this statement. I know that it helps develop people to get them ready for future jobs they may have. ~~and gives experiance~~

[5]

3 Now write only **the opening paragraph** of an article for a teenage magazine expressing your views on the same statement.

I strongly disagree with this statement and I believe you should as well. Work experiance makes people going from being unprepared to face the real working world to being prepared to tackle any job ~~they you~~ you go into.

[5]

Total Marks _____ / 20

Shakespeare

Context and Themes

1 Think about the Shakespeare play you have studied and write a sentence to explain how each of the following aspects of social and historical context is reflected in it.

a) The play's setting — **Example: *Romeo and Juliet* is set in Italy, a country associated with romance and feuding families.**

_____

_____

b) History and politics

_____

_____

c) Religion

_____

d) Society

_____

e) Gender roles

_____

f) Cultural context

_____ [12]

2 Think about the play you have studied and write a sentence explaining how each of the following themes is reflected in it.

a) Marriage — Example: **In *Romeo and Juliet* Capulet sees it as his right and duty to choose Juliet's husband, but Romeo and Juliet see marriage as an expression of love.**

_____

b) Appearance and reality

_____

c) Power

_____

d) Revenge

_____

e) Loyalty and betrayal

_____

f) Parents and children

_____ [12]

Total Marks _____ / 24

Characters, Language and Structure

1. Choose at least three characters from the play you have studied and find quotations (either something they say or something other characters say) which you feel tell us something about their characters.

Enter the characters' names and appropriate quotations, together with a brief explanation of what you think each quotation tells us, in the table below.

If you have studied *The Tempest* you could start with:

Character	Quotation	What it tells us
Caliban	The clouds methought would open and show riches Ready to drop upon me, that when I waked I cried to dream again (Act 3 Scene 2).	An unexpected, sensitive side of Caliban, showing him to be more than a monster.

[12]

2. Below are some quotations from Shakespeare which demonstrate his use of the following literary techniques: metaphor, oxymoron, pathetic fallacy / personification, rhetorical question.

For each one, state which technique is being used and explain its effect.

a) O brawling love, O loving hate (*Romeo and Juliet*, Act 1 Scene 1)

b) But since I am a dog, beware my fangs. (*The Merchant of Venice*, Act 3 Scene 3)

c) Brutus and Caesar: what should be in that 'Caesar?' (*Julius Caesar*, Act 1 Scene 2)

d) The winds did sing it to me [...] and the thunder [...] pronounced / The name of Prosper. (*The Tempest*, Act 3 Scene 3)

	Technique	Effect
a)		
b)		
c)		
d)		

[12]

Total Marks _____ / 24

The Nineteenth-Century Novel

Context and Themes

1 Look at these statements about life in the nineteenth century and write a sentence or two saying whether and how each one is reflected in the novel you have studied.

a) Christianity was part of the fabric of life and writers could assume their readers shared Christian ideas and values.

Example: **In _Great Expectations_, the moral values are those of Christianity. Virtues such as humility, self-sacrifice and love win out over vices like selfishness, greed and dishonesty.**

b) Nineteenth-century Britain was a rich country but many people were extremely poor.

It reflects A christmas carol really well since one of the key themes is wealth and poverty

c) Nineteenth-century women had far fewer rights than men and a more limited role in society.

d) The nineteenth century was a time of discovery, adventure and scientific advances.

e) Nineteenth-century writers wrote about both personal feelings and moral responsibility.

[10]

2 a) On a separate piece of paper, write down some themes that occur in the novel you have studied. Try to find five. Here are some examples to get you started:

Pride and Prejudice	social class
Frankenstein	nature and nurture
A Christmas Carol	poverty
Jane Eyre	integrity
Great Expectations	friendship
The Strange Case of Dr Jekyll and Mr Hyde	hypocrisy

[5]

b) Now write a sentence or two about each of these themes, for example:

In _Pride and Prejudice_ awareness of social class can lead to misunderstanding and unhappiness, as well as being a source of humour.

[10]

Total Marks _____ / 25

The Nineteenth-Century Novel

1 Identify the main characters in your novel and draw up a chart for each like the one below:
Try to complete charts for five characters.

Name	*Ebernizer Scrooge*
Background	
Personality	*Selfish, miserly, horrible*
Relationships	
Motivation	*Only cares about his money*
Function	

[25]

2 Below are five quotations from nineteenth-century novels (**a–e**) and five descriptions of their use of language (**v–z**). Match each quotation to the appropriate description.

a) It is a truth universally acknowledged that a single man in possession of a good fortune must be in want of a wife. *Pride and Prejudice*, Chapter 1	**v)** The writer uses pathetic fallacy to create a mood.
b) Mud-coloured clouds drooped sadly over the muddy streets. *The Sign of Four*, Chapter 3	**w)** The first-person narrator uses a short, simple sentence for impact.
c) I pursued nature to her hiding places. *Frankenstein*, Chapter 4	**x)** The author uses irony to amuse the reader, making a statement that is clearly not true.
d) '…And it were my intentions to have had put upon his tombstone that Whatsume'er the failings on his part, Remember reader he were that good in his hart.' *Great Expectations*, Chapter 5	**y)** The writer uses personification, making an idea more real by writing as if it were a person.
e) Reader, I married him. *Jane Eyre*, Chapter 38	**z)** The writer uses non-standard English to reflect the origins of the speaker and amuse the reader.

[10]

Total Marks _____ / 35

Modern Texts

Context and Themes

1 Think about the social, historical and cultural context of the modern text you have studied. If you have studied the stories in the AQA Anthology, answer on one story. You might want to try further answers on other stories.

a) Write a paragraph describing the 'world' of the prose text you have studied. Include information about when and where it is set, the lifestyle of the characters, their attitudes and the attitudes of society in general.

....

....

....

....

.... **[5]**

b) Write a paragraph explaining how this world differs from the world you live in today.

....

....

....

....

.... **[5]**

c) Now think about when the text was written, its genre and form, and its intended audience. Write a paragraph about how these elements are reflected in the text.

....

....

....

....

.... **[5]**

2 a) In the table below, or on a separate piece of paper, write down some themes that occur in the text you have studied. Try to find four. **[4]**

b) Now write a sentence or two about each theme, for example:

growing up	The young people in 'The Darkness Out There' grow up when they encounter the dark side of adult life in an unlikely place.

[8]

Modern Texts

Characters

1 Identify the main characters in your novel and draw up a chart for each like the one below:

Name	
Background	
Personality	
Relationships	
Motivation	
Function	

[25]

Language and Structure

2 If you have studied a novel or short stories, answer the following questions (**a–e**). If you have studied the stories in the AQA Anthology, answer on one story. You might want to try further answers on other stories.

a) How would you describe the narrator? ....

b) How would you describe the register used by the narrator? ....

c) Have you noticed anything interesting about the way in which any of the characters speak? ....

d) How is your text divided? ....

e) Give an example of the use of figurative language from your text. ....
....

If you have studied a play, answer these questions (**f–j**):

f) What, if anything, do we learn from the stage directions? ....
....

g) Do any of the characters speak directly to the audience? If so, which ones and why? ....
....

h) Are there any interesting differences between the ways in which characters speak? ....
....

i) How is the play divided? ....

j) Give an example of the use of figurative language from your text.
....
....

[10]

Total Marks .... / 35

Poetry

Context and Themes

Context

Think about the social, historical and cultural context of the poems you have studied. If you have studied the 'Love and Relationships' cluster, answer question 1. If you have studied 'Power and Conflict', answer question 2.

1 Match these descriptions of the context of poems to the appropriate poems.

    a) This poem is rooted in the poet's Irish heritage. ....

    b) The poem's language reflects the speaker's Asian heritage. ....

    c) The poet uses a Petrarchan sonnet to express her feelings. .... [3]

2 Match these descriptions of poems' context to the appropriate poems.

    a) In this Romantic poem the poet learns from nature. *The prelude*

    b) This poem reflects on the Japanese experience of the Second World War.
                Kamikaze

    c) This poem considers the effect of his experiences on a soldier who has just returned
    from war. *Remains* .... [3]

Themes

Now think about themes and ideas touched on in the poems you have studied. If you have studied the 'Love and Relationships' cluster, answer question 3. If you have studied 'Power and Conflict', answer question 4.

3 Which poems touch on the following aspects of the main theme (love and relationships)? Try to find at least three for each. You may list the same poem under more than one heading:

a) Parent/child relationships	
b) Loveless relationships	
c) Identity	
d) Lasting romantic love	

[12]

4 Which poems touch on the following aspects of the main theme (power and conflict)? Try to find at least three for each. You may list the same poem under more than one heading:

a) The experience of combatants (soldiers)	*The charge of the light brigade* *Bayonet charge kamikaze*
b) The effect of war on non-combatants	*War photographer Poppies* *The Emigree*
c) The abuse of power	*Ozymandias My last Duchess London*
d) Memories	*Remains Remains Poppies Kamikaze*

[12]

Total Marks .... / 30

Language, Form and Structure

1 Below are some lines taken from poems which demonstrate poets' use of various language choices and literary techniques. Some are taken from 'Love and Relationships' and some from 'Power and Conflict'.

a) And a few leaves lay on the starving sod;   ('Neutral Tones')

b) Long, long shall I rue thee   ('When We Two Parted')

c) the waterlogged earth
gulping for breath at our feet   ('Winter Swans')

d) years between us. Anchor. Kite   ('Mother, any distance')

e) Dem tell me bout de man who discover de balloon
And de cow who jump over de moon   ('Checking Out Me History')

f) The only light is red and softly glows,
as though this were a church   ('War Photographer')

g) …, the flung spray hits
The very windows, spits like a tame cat   ('Storm on the Island')

Some of the techniques below are used in more than one of these quotations, and some quotations include more than one technique. State which techniques are being used and explain their effect.

alliteration   archaic language   assonance   caesura   dialect   end-stopping   enjambment metaphor   pathetic fallacy/personification   repetition   rhyming couplet   simile   onomatopoeia

	Technique	Effect
a)		
b)		
c)		
d)		
e)		
f)		
g)		

[40]

Total Marks _____ / 40

Poetry

Unseen Poetry

1. Read the poem below and answer the questions that follow. (Use a separate piece of paper if necessary.)

Storm in the Black Forest, D. H. Lawrence

Now it is almost night, from the bronzey soft sky
jugfull after jugfull of pure white liquid fire, bright white
tipples over and spills down,
and is gone
and gold-bronze flutters bent through the thick upper air.

And as the electric liquid pours out, sometimes
a still brighter white snake wriggles among it, spilled
and tumbling wriggling down the sky:
and then the heavens cackle with uncouth sounds.

And the rain won't come, the rain refuses to come!

This is the electricity that man is supposed to have mastered
chained, subjugated to his use!
supposed to!

---

a) Where and when is it set?...

....

b) Is there a strong regular rhythm or rhyme scheme? If so, what effect does it have? If not, what effect does this have?...

c) Give an example of alliteration and explain its effect..

....

d) Give an example of assonance and explain its effect..

....

e) Give an example of the use of metaphor and explain its effect. ....

....

f) Explain the poet's repeated use of 'and'...

....

g) What is the significance of the final line 'supposed to!'?...

....

h) What do you think the poem is really about?...

i) How does the storm make the poet feel?..

j) How does the poem make you feel?... [20]

Total Marks .... / 20

Poetry

2 Read this poem. (Note that this poem is one stanza.)

The Vixen, John Clare

Among the taller wood with ivy hung,
The old fox plays and dances round her young.
She snuffs and barks if any passes by
And swings her tail and turns prepared to fly.
The horseman hurries by, she bolts to see,
And turns agen, from danger never free.
If any stands she runs among the poles

And barks and snaps and drives them in the holes.
The shepherd sees them and the boy goes by
And gets a stick and progs the hole to try.
They get all still and lie in safety sure,
And out again when everything's secure,
And start and snap at blackbirds bouncing by
To fight and catch the great white butterfly.

Re-read the poem on page 31 and compare the two poems using the chart below.

	'Storm in the Black Forest'	'The Vixen'
Setting (time and place)		The poem takes place in the woods on what seems to be a typical day for the vixen.
What happens in the poem		
Structure		
Rhythm and rhyme		
Vocabulary/register		
Use of sound		
Imagery		
Themes and poet's attitude		

[32]

Total Marks .... / 32

English Language Paper 1

Explorations in Creative Reading and Writing

You should spend a total of 1 hour 45 minutes on this paper.
You are advised to spend about 15 minutes reading through the source and all five questions.
Answer **all** questions.
The marks for questions are shown in brackets.
There are 40 marks for **Section A** (reading) and 40 marks for **Section B** (writing). The maximum mark for this paper is 80.

Source A

This extract is the opening of 'The Invisible Man', a short detective story by G. K. Chesterton, first published in 1911.

In the cool blue twilight of two steep streets in Camden Town, the shop at the corner, a confectioner's,[1] glowed like the butt of a cigar. One should rather say, perhaps, like the butt of a firework, for the light was of many colours and some complexity, broken up by many mirrors and dancing on many gilt and gaily-coloured cakes and sweetmeats. Against this one fiery glass
5 were glued the noses of many gutter-snipes,[2] for the chocolates were all wrapped in those red and gold and green metallic colours which are almost better than chocolate itself; and the huge white wedding-cake in the window was somehow at once remote and satisfying, just as if the whole North Pole were good to eat. Such rainbow provocations could naturally collect the youth of the neighbourhood up to the ages of ten or twelve. But this corner was also attractive to youth at a
10 later stage; and a young man, not less than twenty-four, was staring into the same shop window. To him, also, the shop was of fiery charm, but this attraction was not wholly to be explained by chocolates; which, however, he was far from despising.

He was a tall, burly, red-haired young man, with a resolute face but a listless manner. He carried under his arm a flat, grey portfolio of black-and-white sketches, which he had sold with more
15 or less success to publishers ever since his uncle (who was an admiral) had disinherited him for Socialism, because of a lecture which he had delivered against that economic theory. His name was John Turnbull Angus.

Entering at last, he walked through the confectioner's shop to the back room, which was a sort of pastry-cook restaurant, merely raising his hat to the young lady who was serving there. She
20 was a dark, elegant, alert girl in black, with a high colour and very quick, dark eyes; and after the ordinary interval she followed him into the inner room to take his order.

His order was evidently a usual one. 'I want, please,' he said with precision, 'one halfpenny bun and a small cup of black coffee.' An instant before the girl could turn away he added, 'Also, I want you to marry me.'

[1] *confectioner* – a maker or seller of sweets and pastries

[2] *gutter-snipes* – 'street' children

Section A: Reading

Answer **all** questions in this section.
You are advised to spend about 45 minutes on this section.

1 Read again the first paragraph of Source A.

   List four things that can be seen through the window of the confectioner's shop.   **[4 marks]**

2 Look in detail at this extract from the first paragraph of the source (lines 1–9).

> In the cool blue twilight of two steep streets in Camden Town, the shop at the corner, a
> confectioner's, glowed like the butt of a cigar. One should rather say, perhaps, like the butt of
> a firework, for the light was of many colours and some complexity, broken up by many mirrors
> and dancing on many gilt and gaily-coloured cakes and sweetmeats. Against this one fiery glass
> were glued the noses of many gutter-snipes, for the chocolates were all wrapped in those red and
> gold and green metallic colours which are almost better than chocolate itself; and the huge white
> wedding-cake in the window was somehow at once remote and satisfying, just as if the whole
> North Pole were good to eat. Such rainbow provocations could naturally collect the youth of the
> neighbourhood up to the ages of ten or twelve.

   How does the writer use language to describe how attractive the shop window is to children?

   You could include the writer's choice of:
   • words and phrases
   • language features and techniques
   • sentence forms.   **[8 marks]**

3 Now think about the whole of the source.

   This text is the opening of a short story.

   How has the writer structured the text to interest you as a reader?

   You could write about:
   • what the writer focuses your attention on at the beginning
   • how and why the writer changes this focus as the extract develops
   • any other structural features that interest you.   **[8 marks]**

4 Focus this answer on the latter part of the source, from line 9 ('But this corner was also attractive to youth at a later stage') to the end.

   How does the writer bring to life the two characters, making the reader interested in them and their story?

   In your response you should:
   • write about your impressions of the characters.
   • evaluate how the writer has created those impressions.
   • support your opinions with quotations from the text.   **[20 marks]**

Section B: Writing

You are advised to spend about 45 minutes on this section.
You are reminded of the need to plan your answer.
You should write in full sentences.
Leave enough time to check your work at the end.

5   You are going to enter a creative writing competition, judged by people of your own age.

EITHER

Write a description suggested by this picture.

OR

Write the opening of a story about a student who is doing a holiday job in a shop or cafe.

[24 marks for content and organization and 16 marks for technical accuracy]

[40 marks]

English Language Paper 2

Writers' Viewpoints and Perspectives

You should spend a total of 1 hour 45 minutes on this paper.
You are advised to spend about 15 minutes reading through the sources and all five questions.
Answer **all** questions.
The marks for questions are shown in brackets.
There are 40 marks for **Section A** (reading) and 40 marks for **Section B** (writing). The maximum mark for the paper is 80.

Source A

SAVE OUR LIBRARY

Local writer joins the fight against closure

By our Arts and Education Correspondent, Alfie Witherspoon

The campaign to save King's Park Library from closure has the backing of an array of local talent. Children's writer Mandy Frobisher says that without the library she would never have become a writer.

'I can't tell you how much that library meant to me,' she told me. 'It gave me a refuge, a place to do my homework, access to centuries of learning and a lifelong love of literature. It made me who I am.
5   Why should today's children be deprived of the opportunities which our generation took for granted?'

Actor Steve Gomez agrees wholeheartedly. 'When I was growing up, the library was the centre of our community. People from all walks of life and all ages used it. They still do. If it closes, there'll be a black hole at the heart of King's Park.' Steve may not mean this literally, but other locals are concerned about what will happen to the building itself, a purpose-built, generously proportioned,
10 roomy building beautifully decorated in the style of the Edwardian Arts and Crafts movement.

Campaigners have high hopes that the backing of Mary and Steve, and other well-known local figures, will help to publicize their campaign and maybe even persuade the Mayor and council to change their minds.

However, a spokesperson for the council claims that the facts simply don't justify keeping the
15 library open. Statistics show that there are now fewer than 300 regular borrowers, almost all of them pensioners, and that number is falling all the time. Figures for people using the references facilities are equally depressing, with only a handful of knowledge-seekers using the facilities each day.

Nevertheless, campaign leader Councillor Laurel Tompkins says she will continue to fight the closure 'every inch of the way'. According to her, the savings to be made by shutting King's Park
20 and five other local libraries are 'a drop in the ocean'. She acknowledges the government has made cuts in its funding – and that King's Park isn't the thriving, populous area it once was – but is convinced that it is not worth devastating the community for a comparatively small saving. 'And when new research is showing that one in three children in the UK does not own a book,' she adds, 'how can the Mayor deprive our kids of the chance of borrowing one and being turned on to
25 reading for life?'

Source B

A letter to *The Times*, written in 1891, about a vote on the issues of public libraries in the London district of Marylebone. Under the Public Libraries Act, people had to vote in favour of public libraries before they could be built by a local council. This letter is from representatives of a group that was running free libraries without public funding.

PUBLIC LIBRARIES IN MARYLEBONE: TO THE EDITOR OF *THE TIMES*

Sir,– May we be allowed, through your columns, to appeal to the ratepayers[1] of Marylebone to record their votes at the end of the present week in favour of the adoption of the Public Libraries Acts, and thus secure for this large and wealthy parish the inestimable social advantages of good libraries, free to all classes, in every district?

5   We do not make this appeal in order to expatiate upon these advantages, because, with free libraries springing up in all directions, they are generally admitted. We would rather remind Marylebone of the work which our voluntary association has accomplished during the last three years – a work which must, in all probability, be brought to an end within the next year or so, unless the financial burden of maintaining the existing voluntary libraries be transferred from our association to the ratepayers at large.

10   The history of the Marylebone Free Library movement is briefly this:– An effort was made in 1887 to obtain sufficient funds, £20,000, to erect a handsome central library, which should not only be a permanent Jubilee[2] memorial, but also serve as a stimulus to the inhabitants of Marylebone to adopt the Public Libraries Acts. The movement failed, only about £7,000 being promised, and an appeal to the ratepayers the following year failed also, not so much from opposition as from apathy on the part of the inhabitants. Our association, in no wise daunted, decided to establish small local reading rooms and libraries in two of the most populous parts of the

15 parish, in the hope that by these object-lessons demonstration amounting to proof would be given both of a great social need and a successful means of meeting it. We have not been mistaken in our calculations. The library in Lisson-grove, opened in 1889, has been an extraordinary success. The space is limited, and accommodation plain and insufficient, but notwithstanding these drawbacks no less than 219,000 persons of all sorts and conditions have used the news and reading room and the reference and lending libraries during the past year. A carefully

20 selected library of 4,000 volumes has attracted 1,200 borrowers, whilst the demand increases daily. Our second library in Mortimer-street, nearly opposite the Middlesex Hospital, was only opened nine months ago and is on a smaller scale. Its success, however, is proportionately greater. Funds, and funds only, are required to enable the association to multiply these useful institutions. One library is £300 in debt, and the funds of the second are running low. Unfortunately, many of our actual and also many of our would-be subscribers feel that the very

25 success of our movement relieves them of individual responsibility. That which exists, they say, for the good of all should be paid for by all, more especially when the maximum amount imposed upon each ratepayer by the 1d. rate[3] is so trifling. During the past few years no less than 28 metropolitan and suburban districts, some poor, some rich, have adopted the Public Libraries Acts. Others are about to follow, and our association hopes that Marylebone will be of the number. Much want of knowledge and indifference still exist on the subject of free

30 libraries, and we therefore appeal to you to give publicity to our case, and thus contribute to success at the poll.

We beg, Sir, to remain yours obediently,

JOHN R. HOLLOND Chairman

FRANK DEBENHAM Treasurer

Marylebone Public Libraries Association, 18 Baker-street. March 4.

[1] *ratepayers* – people who pay 'rates' or local taxes, the equivalent of Council Tax today
[2] *Jubilee* – the golden jubilee of Queen Victoria had taken place in 1887
[3] *1d. rate* – a one -penny tax; local councils could increase rates by up to a penny per pound for libraries and museums.

Practice Exam Papers

Section A: Reading

Answer **all** questions in this section.
You are advised to spend about 45 minutes on this section.

1   Read again **Source A** from lines 1 to 13.

Choose four statements below which are TRUE.

- Shade the boxes of the ones that you think are true.
- Choose a maximum of four statements.

A. King's Park Library is threatened with closure ☐

B. Mandy Frobisher writes for children. ☐

C. Steve Gomez is in favour of closing the library. ☐

D. There is a big hole in the middle of the park. ☐

E. The campaigners have given up hope. ☐

F. Frobisher used to do her homework in the library. ☐

G. Nobody in King's Park has heard of Mandy Frobisher or Steve Gomez. ☐

H. Gomez thinks the whole community benefits from the library. ☐

[4 marks]

2   You need to refer to **Source A** and **Source B** for this question.

Use details from **both** sources. Write a summary of the differences between King's Park Library now and the two Marylebone libraries in 1891.   **[8 marks]**

3   You now need to refer **only** to **Source B**, the letter written by John Hollond and Frank Debenham to *The Times*.

How do the writers use language to try to influence the reader?   **[12 marks]**

4 For this question you need to refer to **both Source A** and **Source B**.

Compare how the writers convey different attitudes to libraries.

In your answer you should:

- Compare the different attitudes (both those of the writers themselves and those that they report).
- Compare the methods they use to convey these attitudes.
- Support your ideas with quotations from both texts.   **[16 marks]**

Section B: Writing

You are advised to spend about 45 minutes on this section.
You are reminded of the need to plan your answer.
You should write in full sentences.
You should leave enough time to check your work at the end.

5 'Libraries are a thing of the past. You can get all the information you need from the internet at home. People who like books can buy them or download them. There are much more important things to spend public money on.'

Write an article for a broadsheet newspaper in which you explain your point of view on this statement.

[24 marks for content and organization; 16 marks for technical accuracy]

[40 marks]

Practice Exam Papers

English Literature Paper 1

Shakespeare and the Nineteenth-Century Novel

You should spend a total of 1 hour 45 minutes on this paper.
Answer one question from Section A and one from Section B.
The maximum mark for the paper is 64.
Spelling, punctuation and grammar will be assessed in Section A. There are four marks available
for AO4 in addition to 30 marks for answering the question.
There are 30 marks for Section B.

Section A

Shakespeare	Question	Page
Macbeth	1	41
Romeo and Juliet	2	41
The Tempest	3	42
The Merchant of Venice	4	43
Much Ado About Nothing	5	43
Julius Caesar	6	44

Section B

The nineteenth-century novel		Question	Page
Robert Louis Stevenson	*The Strange Case of Dr Jekyll and Mr Hyde*	7	45
Charles Dickens	*A Christmas Carol*	8	45
Charles Dickens	*Great Expectations*	9	46
Charlotte Brontë	*Jane Eyre*	10	46
Mary Shelley	*Frankenstein*	11	47
Jane Austen	*Pride and Prejudice*	12	47
Sir Arthur Conan Doyle	*The Sign of Four*	13	48

Section A: Shakespeare

Answer **one** question from this section on your chosen text.

1 *Macbeth*

Read the following extract from Act 5, Scene 5 of *Macbeth* and then answer the question that follows.

Here, Macbeth is preparing to meet the invading armies of Malcolm and Macduff.

> MACBETH   I have almost forgot the taste of fears.
> The time has been my senses would have cooled
> To hear the night-shriek, and my fell of hair
> Would at a dismal treatise rise and stir
> As life were in't. I have supped full with horrors.
> Direness, familiar to my slaughterous thoughts,
> Cannot once start me.
>
> *Enter Seyton*
>
>   Wherefore was that cry?
>
> SEYTON   The Queen, my lord, is dead.
>
> MACBETH   She should have died hereafter.
> There would have been a time for such a word.
> Tomorrow, and tomorrow, and tomorrow
> Creeps in this petty pace from day to day
> To the last syllable of recorded time,
> And all our yesterdays have lighted fools
> The way to dusty death. Out, out, brief candle.
> Life's but a walking shadow, a poor player
> That struts and frets his hour upon the stage,
> And then is heard no more. It is a tale
> Told by an idiot, full of sound and fury,
> Signifying nothing.

Starting with this extract, explore how Shakespeare presents Macbeth's changing character.

Write about:
- how Shakespeare presents Macbeth in this speech
- how Shakespeare presents Macbeth in the play as a whole.   **[30 marks + AO4 4 marks]**

2 *Romeo and Juliet*

Read the following extract from Act 3, Scene 5 of *Romeo and Juliet* and then answer the question that follows.

Here, Romeo is leaving Juliet's room the morning after their secret wedding.

> JULIET   Wilt thou be gone? It is not yet near day.
> It was the nightingale, and not the lark,

	That pierced the fear-full hollow of thine ear.
	Nightly she sings on yon pomegranate tree.
	Believe me, love, it was the nightingale.
ROMEO	It was the lark, the herald of the morn,
	No nightingale. Look, love, what envious streaks
	Do lace the severing clouds in yonder east.
	Night's candles are burnt out, and jocund day
	Stands tiptoe on the misty mountain tops.
	I must be gone and live, or stay and die.
JULIET	Yon light is not daylight; I know it, I.
	It is some meteor that the sun exhaled
	To be to thee this night a torchbearer
	And light thee on thy way to Mantua.
	Therefore stay yet. Thou need'st not be gone.

Starting with this extract, write about how Shakespeare presents ideas about love and marriage in *Romeo and Juliet*.

Write about:
- how Shakespeare presents Romeo and Juliet's relationship in this extract
- how Shakespeare presents ideas about love and marriage
  in the whole play.   **[30 marks + AO4 4 marks]**

3 *The Tempest*

Read the following extract from Act 4, Scene 1 of *The Tempest* and then answer the question that follows.

In this scene Prospero punishes Caliban and his companions for plotting to kill him.

A noise of hunters is heard. Enter spirits in the shape of dogs and hounds. They hunt Caliban, Stefano and Trinculo, Prospero and Ariel setting them on

PROSPERO	Hey, Mountain, hey!
ARIEL	Silver! There it goes, Silver!
PROSPERO	Fury, Fury! There, Tyrant, there! Hark, hark!

Exeunt Stefano, Trinculo and Caliban, pursued by spirits

	Go, charge my goblins that they grind their joints
	With dry convulsions, shorten up their sinews
	With aged cramps, and shall more pinch-spotted make them
	Than pard or cat o' mountain.
Cries within	
ARIEL	Hark, they roar!
PROPSERO	Let them be hunted soundly. At this hour
	Lies at my mercy all mine enemies.
	Shortly shall all my labours end, and thou
	Shalt have the air at freedom. For a little,
	Follow, and do me service.

Starting with this extract, explain how Shakespeare writes about revenge and forgiveness in *The Tempest*.

Write about:
- how Shakespeare presents ideas about revenge and forgiveness in this extract
- how Shakespeare presents ideas about revenge and forgiveness in the play as a whole.

[30 marks + AO4 4 marks]

4 *The Merchant of Venice*

Read the following extract from Act 3, Scne 3 of *The Merchant of Venice* and then answer the question that follows.

Shylock has had Antonio put in prison for failing to repay the money he lent him.

SHYLOCK	Jailer, look to him. Tell me not of mercy.
	This is the fool that lent the money gratis.
	Jailer, look to him.
ANTONIO	Hear me yet, good Shylock.
SHYLOCK	I'll have my bond. Speak not against my bond.
	I have sworn an oath that I will have my bond.
	Thou called'st me a dog before thou hadst a cause,
	But since I am a dog, beware my fangs.
	The Duke shall grant me justice. I do wonder,
	Thou naughty jailer, that thou art so fond
	To come abroad with him at his request.
ANTONIO	I pray thee hear me speak.
SHYLOCK	I'll have my bond. I will not hear thee speak.
	I'll have my bond, and therefore speak not me more.
	I'll not be made a soft and dull-eyed fool
	To shake the head, relent, and sigh, and yield
	To Christian intercessors. Follow not.
	I'll have no speaking. I will have my bond.

Starting with this extract, write about how Shakespeare presents Shylock as an outsider.

Write about:
- how Shakespeare presents Shylock as an outsider in this extract
- how Shakespeare presents Shylock as an outsider in the play as a whole. **[30 marks + AO4 4 marks]**

5 *Much Ado About Nothing*

Read the following extract from Act 1, Scene 1 of *Much Ado About Nothing* and then answer the question that follows.

The messenger has brought the news that Don Pedro is coming to Messina. Beatrice has asked him whether Benedick is with him.

LEONATO	Faith, niece, you tax Signor Benedick too much. But he'll be meet with you,
	I doubt it not.
MESSENGER	He hath done good service, lady, in these wars.

BEATRICE	You had musty victual, and he hath holp to eat it. He is a very valiant trencherman, he hath an excellent stomach.
MESSENGER	And a good soldier too, lady.
BEATRICE	And a good soldier to a lady, but what is he to a lord?
MESSENGER	A lord to a lord, a man to a man, stuffed with all honourable virtues.
BEATRICE	It is so, indeed. He is no less than a stuffed man. But for the stuffing – well, we are all mortal.
LEONATO	You must not, sir, mistake my niece. There is a kind of merry war betwixt Signor Benedick and her. They never meet but there's a skirmish of wit between them.

Starting with this extract, how does Shakespeare present the relationship between Benedick and Beatrice?

Write about:
• how Shakespeare presents their relationship in the extract
• how he presents their relationship in the whole of the play.   **[30 marks + AO4 4 marks]**

6 | *Julius Caesar*

Read the following extract from Act 2, Scene 1 of *Julius Caesar* and then answer the question that follows.

Portia is concerned that her husband, Brutus, is keeping secrets from her.

BRUTUS	You are my true and honourable wife,
	As dear to me as are the ruddy drops
	That visit my sad heart.
PORTIA	If this were true, then should I know this secret.
	I grant I am a woman, but withal
	A woman that Lord Brutus took to wife.
	I grant I am a woman, but withal
	A woman well reputed, Cato's daughter.
	Think you I am no stronger than my sex,
	Being so fathered and so husbanded?
	Tell me your counsels; I will not disclose 'em.
	I have made strong proof of my constancy,
	Giving myself a voluntary wound
	Here in the thigh. Can I bear that with patience,
	And not my husband's secrets?
BRUTUS	O ye gods,
	Render me worthy of this noble wife!

Starting with this extract, explore how Shakespeare presents women and their role in *Julius Caesar*.

Write about:
• how Shakespeare writes about women in this speech
• how Shakespeare writes about women in the play as a whole.   **[30 marks + AO4 4 marks]**

Section B: The Nineteenth-Century Novel

Answer the question on the novel you have studied.

7 **Robert Louis Stevenson:** *The Strange Case of Dr Jekyll and Mr Hyde*

Answer both parts of the question.

Re-read Chapter 8 ('The Last Night') from

> 'That's it!' said Poole. 'It was this way. I came suddenly into the theatre from the garden. It seems he had slipped out to look for this drug or whatever it is; for the cabinet door was open, and there he was at the far end of the room digging among the crates…'

to

> '…No, sir, that thing in the mask was never Doctor Jekyll – God knows what it was but it was never Doctor Jekyll; and it is the belief of my heart that there was murder done.'

In this extract, Poole, Dr Jekyll's servant, is telling Mr Utterson why he thinks that Jekyll has been murdered.

Starting with this extract, write about how Stevenson uses Jekyll's transformation to explore ideas about good and evil in *The Strange Case of Dr Jekyll and Mr Hyde*.

Write about:
- how Stevenson writes about what Poole has seen in this extract
- how he uses the transformation to explore ideas about good and evil in the novel as a whole.

[30 marks]

8 **Charles Dickens:** *A Christmas Carol*

Answer both parts of the question.

Re-read Stave (Chapter) 3 ('The Second of the Three Spirits') from

> 'Forgive me if I am not justified in what I ask,' said Scrooge, looking intently at the Spirit's robe, 'but I see something strange, and not belonging to yourself, protruding from your skirts. Is it a foot or a claw?'

to

> 'Are there no prisons?' said the Spirit, turning on him for the last time with his own words. 'Are there no workhouses?'

In this extract, the children Ignorance and Want are revealed to Scrooge by the Ghost of Christmas Present. Starting with this extract, explain how Dickens writes about social problems in *A Christmas Carol*.

Write about:
- how Dickens writes about social problems in this extract
- how he explore ideas about social problems and social responsibility in the novel as a whole.

[30 marks]

9 **Charles Dickens:** *Great Expectations*

Answer both parts of the question.

Re-read Chapter 1 from

> Ours was the marsh country, down by the river, within, as the river wound, twenty miles of the sea. My first most vivid and broad impression of the identity of things, seems to me to have been gained on a memorable raw afternoon towards evening.

to

> I earnestly expressed my hope that he wouldn't, and held tighter to the tombstone on which he had put me; partly, to keep myself upon it; partly, to keep myself from crying.

In this extract, Pip meets the convict, Magwitch, for the first time.

Starting with this extract, write about how Dickens uses Pip as a narrator.

Write about:
- how Pip describes his encounter with Magwitch in this extract
- Pip's role as narrator in the novel as a whole.

[30 marks]

10 **Charlotte Brontë:** *Jane Eyre*

Answer both parts of the question.

Re-read Chapter 15 from

> And was Mr Rochester now ugly in my eyes?

to

> Suppose he should be absent spring, summer, and autumn: how joyless sunshine and fine days will seem!

In this extract, Jane reflects on Mr Rochester's character, just before fire breaks out at Thornfield.

Starting with this extract, write about how Brontë presents the character of Mr Rochester and Jane's changing feelings towards him.

Write about:
- how Brontë writes about Rochester and Jane's feelings towards him in this extract
- how Brontë writes about Rochester and Jane's feelings towards him in the novel as a whole.

[30 marks]

11 **Mary Shelley:** *Frankenstein*

Answer both parts of the question.

Re-read Chapter 7 from

> We were soon joined by Elizabeth. Time had altered her since I last beheld her; it had endowed her with loveliness surpassing the beauty of her childish years.

to

> 'Dearest niece,' said my father, 'dry your tears. If she is, as you believe, innocent, rely on the justice of our laws, and the activity with which I shall prevent the slightest shadow of partiality.'

In this extract, Elizabeth, Victor Frankenstein and his father discuss the innocence of Justine, who has been arrested for murder.

Starting with this extract, write about how Shelley writes about attitudes to women.

Write about:
- how Shelley writes about women in this extract
- how Shelley writes about women and attitudes to women in the novel as a whole.   **[30 marks]**

12 **Jane Austen:** *Pride and Prejudice*

Answer both parts of the question.

Re-read Chapter 20 from

> 'An unhappy alternative is before you, Elizabeth. From this day you must be a stranger to one of your parents. – Your mother will never see you again if you do *not* marry Mr Collins, and I will never see you again if you *do*.'

to

> 'But I tell you what, Miss Lizzy, if you take it into your head to go on refusing every offer of marriage in this way, you will never get a husband at all – and I am sure I do not know who is to maintain you when your father is dead.'

In this extract, Elizabeth has just refused Mr Collins's proposal of marriage.

Starting with this extract, explore how Austen writes about attitudes to marriage in *Pride and Prejudice*.

Write about:
- how Austen writes about marriage in this extract
- how Austen writes about attitudes to marriage in the novel as a whole.   **[30 marks]**

13 **Sir Arthur Conan Doyle:** *The Sign of Four*

Answer both parts of the question.

Re-read Chapter 5 from

> 'There is something devilish in this, Watson,' said he, more moved than I had ever before seen him. 'What do you make of it?'

to

> In the light of the lantern I read, with a thrill of horror, 'The sign of the four'.

In this extract, Holmes and Watson discover the body of the murdered man, Bartholomew Sholto, at Pondicherry Lodge.

Starting with this extract, explore how Conan Doyle writes about murder in *The Sign of Four*.

Write about:
* how Conan Doyle writes about murder in this extract
* how Conan Doyle writes about murder in the novel as a whole. **[30 marks]**

English Literature Paper 2

Modern Texts and Poetry

You should spend a total of 2 hours 15 minutes on this paper.
Answer **one** question from **Section A, one** from **Section B** and **both** questions in **Section C**.
The marks for questions are shown in brackets.
The maximum mark for the paper is 96.
AO4 (Spelling, punctuation and grammar) will be assessed in Section A. There are four marks available
for AO4 in addition to 30 marks for answering the question. AO4 assesses the following skills: Use a range of vocabulary and sentence
structures for clarity, purpose and effect, with accurate spelling and punctuation.
There are 30 marks for **Section B** and 32 marks for **Section C**.

Section A

Modern prose or drama		Questions	Page
J. B. Priestley	*An Inspector Calls*	1–2	50
Willy Russell	*Blood Brothers*	3–4	50
Alan Bennett	*The History Boys*	5–6	50
Dennis Kelly	*DNA*	7–8	51
Simon Stephens	*The Curious Incident of the Dog in the Night-Time*	9–10	51
Shelagh Delaney	*A Taste of Honey*	11–12	51
William Golding	*Lord of the Flies*	13–14	52
AQA Anthology	*Telling Tales*	15–16	52
George Orwell	*Animal Farm*	17–18	52
Kazuo Ishiguro	*Never Let Me Go*	19–20	53
Meera Syal	*Anita and Me*	21–22	53
Stephen Kelman	*Pigeon English*	23–24	53

Section B

Poetry		Question	Page
AQA Anthology	Poems Past and Present		
	Love and Relationships	25	54
	Power and Conflict	26	55

Section C

Unseen texts	Question	Page
	27.1	56
	27.2	56

Practice Exam Papers

Section A: Modern Prose or Drama

Answer **one** question from this section on your chosen text.

J. B. Priestley: *An Inspector Calls*

EITHER

1. What is the significance of Eva Smith in *An Inspector Calls*?

   Write about:
   - what we learn about Eva Smith / Daisy Renton
   - how Priestley uses the 'character' of Eva Smith / Daisy Renton.   **[30 marks + AO4 4 marks]**

OR

2. How does Priestley explore ideas about selfishness in *An Inspector Calls*?

   Write about:
   - the ideas about selfishness in *An Inspector Calls*
   - how Priestley presents these ideas in the way he writes.   **[30 marks + AO4 4 marks]**

Willy Russell: *Blood Brothers*

EITHER

3. How does Russell use the characters of Edward and Mickey to write about social class in *Blood Brothers*?

   Write about:
   - how Russell presents Edward and Mickey
   - how he uses Edward and Mickey to write about social class.   **[30 marks + AO4 4 marks]**

OR

4. How does Russell write about superstition and fate in *Blood Brothers*?

   Write about:
   - ideas about superstition and fate explored in *Blood Brothers*
   - how Russell presents these ideas.   **[30 marks + AO4 4 marks]**

Alan Bennett: *The History Boys*

EITHER

5. How does Bennett present Hector as a teacher in *The History Boys*?

   Write about:
   - what Hector does and says
   - how Bennett presents Hector in the play.   **[30 marks + AO4 4 marks]**

OR

6. How does Bennett explore attitudes to history in *The History Boys*?

   Write about:
   - attitudes to history explored in *The History Boys*
   - how Bennett presents these attitudes.   **[30 marks + AO4 4 marks]**

Dennis Kelly: *DNA*

EITHER

7 How does Kelly write about bullying in *DNA*?

Write about:
* examples of bullying behaviour in *DNA*
* how Kelly presents bullying in the play.   **[30 marks + AO4 4 marks]**

OR

8 How does Kelly present the character of John Tate in *DNA*?

Write about:
* John Tate's behaviour and attitudes
* how Kelly uses John Tate to explore ideas about leadership and responsibility.

[30 marks + AO4 4 marks]

Simon Stephens: *The Curious Incident of the Dog in the Night-Time*

EITHER

9 How does Stephens present the character of Judy as a mother in *The Curious Incident of the Dog in the Night-Time*?

Write about:
* what Judy does and says
* how Stephens presents Judy.   **[30 marks + AO4 4 marks]**

OR

10 How does Stephens present Christopher's experience of education in *The Curious Incident of the Dog in the Night-Time*?

Write about:
* what Christopher's experience of education is and his attitude to it
* how Stephens presents Christopher's experience of education.   **[30 marks + AO4 4 marks]**

Shelagh Delaney: *A Taste of Honey*

EITHER

11 How does Delaney present the character of Jo as a daughter in *A Taste of Honey*?

Write about:
* how Delaney presents the character of Jo
* how Delaney uses the character of Jo to explore parent/child relationships.

[30 marks + AO4 4 marks]

OR

12 How does Delaney write about responsibility in *A Taste of Honey*?

Write about:
* ideas about responsibility in *A Taste of Honey*
* how Delaney presents these ideas.   **[30 marks + AO4 4 marks]**

William Golding: *Lord of the Flies*

EITHER

13 How does Golding present the character of Ralph as a leader in *Lord of the Flies*?

Write about:
- how Golding presents the character of Ralph
- how Golding uses the character of Ralph to explore ideas about leadership.

[30 marks + AO4 4 marks]

OR

14 How does Golding present ideas about the breakdown of civilization in *Lord of the Flies*?

Write about:
- ideas about the breakdown of civilization in *Lord of the Flies*
- how Golding presents these ideas.   **[30 marks + AO4 4 marks]**

AQA Anthology: *Telling Tales*

EITHER

15 How do writers explore ideas about identity in 'The Invisible Mass of the Back Row' and one other story from *Telling Tales*?

Write about:
- ideas about identity in the two stories
- how the writers present these ideas.   **[30 marks + AO4 4 marks]**

OR

16 How do writers use first-person narrators in 'My Polish Teacher's Tie' and one other story from *Telling Tales*?

Write about:
- the narrators in the two stories
- how the writers use these narrators to explore ideas and issues.   **[30 marks + AO4 4 marks]**

George Orwell: *Animal Farm*

EITHER

17 How does Orwell use the character of Boxer to explore ideas about the working class in *Animal Farm*?

Write about:
- how Orwell presents the character of Boxer
- how Orwell uses the character of Boxer to present ideas about the working class.

[30 marks + AO4 4 marks]

OR

18 How does Orwell present ideas about revolution in *Animal Farm*?

Write about:
- ideas about revolution in *Animal Farm*
- how Orwell presents these ideas.   **[30 marks + AO4 4 marks]**

Kazuo Ishiguro: *Never Let Me Go*

EITHER

19 How does Ishiguro present the guardians in *Never Let Me Go*?

Write about:
- the characters of the guardians in *Never Let Me Go*
- how Ishiguro presents the guardians and uses them to explore ideas and issues.

[30 marks + AO4 4 marks]

OR

20 What is the significance of the gallery in *Never Let Me Go*?

Write about:
- what the gallery is and what it represents to the characters in *Never Let Me Go*
- how Ishiguro uses the gallery to explore ideas and issues.   **[30 marks + AO4 4 marks]**

Meera Syal: *Anita and Me*

EITHER

21 How does Syal present racism in *Anita and Me*?

Write about:
- examples of racism in *Anita and Me*
- how Syal shows Meena becoming aware of racism.   **[30 marks + AO4 4 marks]**

OR

22 How does Syal present Nanima and Mrs Worrall as important influences in Meena's life?

Write about:
- the characters of Nanima and Mrs Worrall
- how they are significant in Meena's life.   **[30 marks + AO4 4 marks]**

Stephen Kelman: *Pigeon English*

EITHER

23 How does Kelman present ideas about culture and heritage in *Pigeon English*?

Write about:
- ideas about culture and heritage *Pigeon English*
- how Kelman presents these ideas.   **[30 marks + AO4 4 marks]**

OR

24 How does Kelman present school life in *Pigeon English*?

Write about:
- Harrison's experiences of school and his feelings about school
- how Kelman presents these attitudes and feelings.   **[30 marks + AO4 4 marks]**

Section B: Poetry

Answer **one** question from this section.

AQA Anthology: *Poems Past and Present*

EITHER

25 **Love and Relationships**

Compare the way poets present feelings of love in Sonnet 29 – 'I think of thee!' and **one** other poem from 'Love and Relationships'.

> **Sonnet 29 – 'I think of thee!',** Elizabeth Barrett Browning
>
> I think of thee! – my thoughts do twine and bud
> About thee, as wild vines, about a tree,
> Put out broad leaves, and soon there's nought to see
> Except the straggling green which hides the wood.
> 5   Yet, O my palm tree, be it understood
> I will not have my thoughts instead of thee
> Who art dearer, better! Rather, instantly
> Renew thy presence; as a strong tree should,
> Rustle thy boughs and set thy trunk all bare,
> 10 And let these bands of greenery which insphere thee
> Drop heavily down, – burst, shattered, everywhere!
> Because, in this deep joy to see and hear thee
> And breathe within thy shadow a new air,
> I do not think of thee – I am too near thee.

[30 marks]

OR

26 **Power and Conflict**

Compare the way poets present suffering in 'London' and **one** other poem from 'Power and Conflict'.

London, William Blake

I wander through each chartered street,
Near where the chartered Thames does flow,
And mark in every face I meet
Marks of weakness, marks of woe.

5 In every cry of every man,
In every infant's cry of fear,
In every voice, in every ban,
The mind-forged manacles I hear:

How the chimney-sweeper's cry
10 Every black'ning church appals
And the hapless soldier's sigh
Runs in blood down palace walls.
But most through midnight streets I hear
How the youthful harlot's curse
15 Blasts the new-born infant's tear,
And blights with plague the marriage hearse.

[30 marks]

Section C: Unseen Texts

Answer **both** questions in this section.

Death the Leveller, James Shirley

The glories of our blood and state
    Are shadows, not substantial things;
There is no armour against Fate;
    Death lays his icy hand on kings:
5   Sceptre and Crown
            Must tumble down,
And in the dust be equal made
    With the poor crookèd scythe and spade.

Some men with swords may reap the field,
10   And plant fresh laurels where they kill:
But their strong nerves at last must yield;
    They tame but one another still:
            Early or late
            They stoop to fate,
15 And must give up their murmuring breath
    When they, pale captives, creep to death.

The garlands wither on your brow,
    Then boast no more your mighty deeds!
Upon Death's purple altar now
20   See where the victor-victim bleeds.
            Your heads must come
            To the cold tomb:
Only the actions of the just
    Smell sweet and blossom in their dust.

27.1 In 'Death the Leveller' how does the poet present his feelings about death?   **[24 marks]**

Requiem, Robert Louis Stevenson

Under the wide and starry sky,
Dig the grave and let me lie.
Glad did I live and gladly die,
And I laid me down with a will.

5   This be the verse you gave for me:
Here he lies where he longed to be;
Home is the sailor, home from the sea,
And the hunter home from the hill.

27.2 In both 'Death the Leveller' and 'Requiem' the poets express their feelings about death. What are the similarities and/or differences between the ways the poets present their feelings?

    [8 marks]

Answers

Key Technical Skills: Writing – pages 4–8

Page 4: Spelling

1. a) tomatoes   b) birthdays
   c) soliloquies   d) families
   e) parentheses   [maximum 5]
2. a) **You're** not going out like that. I asked **your** sister to bring it.
   b) **There** are twenty-five people in the class. They have all done **their** homework but **they're** not sitting in the right places.
   c) Turn it off or it will **wear** out. We have no idea **where** it is but **we're** going anyway.
   d) I **passed** him in the street an hour ago. He walked right **past** me as if I wasn't there.
   e) There were only **two** exams **to** sit but that was one **too** many.
   f) If you don't go to the **practice** you'll be left out of the team. If you want to improve you will have to **practise** every day.
        [1] for each correct answer up to a maximum of [15]
3. Last **night** I went to the cinema with my friend Bob and his **father**, Michael. The whole evening was not very **successful**. The cinema was very **crowded** and we had to sit **separately**. Then, it turned out the film was in a **foreign language** and no-one could understand it. I think it was about the **environment**. Afterwards, Michael took us to a **restaurant where** we had pizzas.
        [1] for each correct answer up to a maximum of [10]

Page 5: Punctuation

1. *Great Expectations,* [1] one of the best-known novels by Charles Dickens, [1] is the story of Pip, [1] a boy who grows up in the marshes of Kent. At [1] the beginning of the story he meets an escaped convict in the churchyard where his parents are buried. [1]   [maximum 5]
2. At about ten o'clock [1], we went to Romio's [1] for pizzas. I'm [1] not sure what Bob's [1] pizza topping was but I had ham and pineapple. I wish I hadn't [1] because later on I was sick in Michael's [1] car. It's [1] brand new and I thought he'd [1] be angry but he wasn't [1]. We're [1] not going there again.   [maximum 10]
3. a) Who was that masked man? Nobody knows. b) The cat slept quietly on the mat; the dog slept noisily on the step. c) I don't believe it! That's the first answer I've got. d) Annie deserved the prize: she was the best baker by far. e) Jane and Elizabeth (the two oldest Bennet sisters) get married at the end.
        [1] for each correct answer up to a maximum of [5]

Page 6: Sentence Structure

1. a) complex   b) minor   c) simple
   d) compound   e) simple
        [1] for each correct answer up to a maximum of [5]
2. a) I bought Anna a bunch of flowers because it was her birthday. [1]
   b) He did not finish the race although they gave him a certificate. [1]
   a) and b) could be written with the conjunctions at the beginning of the sentence, but you would then need to add a comma after the first clause.
   c) I kept going until I reached the finishing line. [1]
3. Joey, who was the oldest cat in the street, never left the garden. [1]
4. Walking down the street, I realized I had forgotten my phone. [1]

Page 7: Text Structure and Organization

1. e) Students of Summerfield College have expressed concern about the environment they have to work in. They have a number of complaints.
   c) Jodie Collins, a spokesperson for the students, has had several meetings about the issue with the Principal. Ms Rundle apparently listened to the students' points, but later sent an email claiming that nothing can be done because of lack of funds.
   a) As a result of this, the student body has decided to appeal to the governors. Jodie has written a letter to every governor, setting out the problems as the students see them.
   d) According to this letter, students' health and safety are at risk. Among other things, toilets are not properly cleaned and standards of hygiene in the kitchen leave a lot to be desired.
   b) As yet no replies have been received. The increasingly angry students are starting to consider taking 'direct action'.   [maximum 5]
2. a) When   b) In spite of
   c) subsequently   d) however
   e) Nevertheless   [maximum 5]

Page 8: Standard English and Grammar

1. a) are   b) are   c) were   d) did
   e) has been   f) have done   g) were…had done
        [maximum 7]
2. a) pleaded   b) few   c) got
        [maximum 3]
3. Jo: Hello. How are you? [1]
   Arthur: Well. Very well, thank you. [1]
   Jo: Do you want (*or* would you like) a drink? [1]
   Arthur: May I have two coffees, please? [1]
   Jo: Of course. Where are you sitting? [1]
4. I was **standing** in the street when Frankie **came** over. [1] I gave him a smile and opened **my mouth** to speak. [1] I was **going to** ask him how he **did** in **maths** (*or* mathematics). [1] I **did not say anything**. [1] **As** soon as I **saw** him I knew he **had done well**. [1]

Key Technical Skills: Reading – pages 9–16

Page 9: Explicit Information and Ideas

1. a, c   [maximum 2]
2. **Any four from**: He was very nice looking. He had a fresh-coloured face. He was clean shaven. He had white hair. He wore odd-shaped collars. He wore a top hat.   [maximum 4]

Page 10: Implicit Information and Ideas

1. a, c, d, g   [maximum 4]

Page 11: Synthesis and Summary

1. a) Trees stand behind the shed. [1] b) Charlotte Green ate Lydia's chocolate. [1] c) Tell me who did it. [1]
2. b, c, f, g, h   [maximum 5]
3. The summary below is a suggestion only. You should have included details of where and when it happened, and a description of the men.
        [1] for each point up to a maximum of [12].

   At nine o'clock on Monday I was in Arbuckle Lane. As I passed number eighteen, I heard a noise. There were two men on the step. One was breaking the glass in the door with something in his hand. I shouted and they turned. One was about six foot, with a grey beard. The other was stocky with curly black hair. The tall man dropped something and they ran.

Page 12: Synthesis and Summary

1.

Mary Jane	Sarah
Parents did not see the point of school	Mother thought education important
Loved going to school	Did not like going to school
40 in a class	24 in class
(Everyone) worked hard	Did not do much work
Teacher very strict	Teacher never told anyone off
Sat in rows	Sat in groups
Not allowed to talk	Talked all the time
Liked the teacher	Did not like the teacher
Respected the teacher	Did not respect the teacher
Appreciated/valued school	Did not appreciate/value school

[1] for each pair up to a maximum of **[10]**

2. Look at the mark scheme below, decide which description is closest to your answer and then decide what mark to give it up to a maximum of **[8]**.

Marks	Skills
7–8	You have given a perceptive interpretation of both texts. You have synthesized evidence from the texts. You have used appropriate quotations from both texts.
5–6	You have started to interpret both texts. You have shown clear connections between texts. You have used relevant quotations from both texts.

Page 13: Referring to the Text

1. a–e, b–d, c–f   **[maximum 3]**

2. **a)** Macbeth refers to the prophecies as 'happy prologues'. **[2]**
  b) He tells us that one of them has come true: 'I am Thane of Cawdor.' **[2]**
  c) Macbeth asks how the prophecies can be evil when the witches have told the truth:

                                If ill,
    Why hath it given me earnest of success
    Commencing in a truth? **[2]**

3.

Point	Frankenstein's response is negative from the start.
Evidence	Referring to the experiment as a 'catastrophe' and his creation as a 'wretch'
Explanation	suggests that he has rejected the creature and will not try to find any good in it.

[maximum 3]

Page 14: Analysing Language 1

1. **a)** dialectical (also colloquial)   **b)** formal
  c) colloquial   **d)** technical   **[maximum 4]**

2. **a)** adjective   **b)** preposition
  c) conjunction   **d)** (concrete) noun
  e) adverb   **f)** verb   **[maximum 6]**

3. **a)** complex   **b)** Jo, Beth or Amy
  c) passive   **d)** past perfect
  e) third person   **[maximum 5]**

Page 15: Analysing Language 2

1. **a)** Simile. It suggests he ran extremely quickly as the wind travels quickly. **[2]** **b)** Metaphor. It suggests that there are

a lot of insects and that they are dangerous, violent and organized. **[2] c)** Both. 'Heart' is a metaphor for her feelings/emotions. Describing it as cold or frozen suggests that she feels nothing.   **[maximum 6]**

2. **a)** time **b)** fizzed/crackled   **[maximum 2]**

3. Look at the mark scheme below, decide which description is closest to your answer and then decide what mark to give it up to a maximum of **[8]**.

Marks	Skills	Examples of possible content
7–8	You have analysed the effects of the choice of language. You have used an appropriate range of quotations. You have used sophisticated subject terminology appropriately.	The opening, which gives a date followed by a minor sentence describing the weather, gives the impression of a diary entry. This will clearly be an account of the narrator's private thoughts. His evocative description of the 'dull' and 'dreary' landscape uses pathetic fallacy (the boulders have 'faces') to imply his own 'melancholy'. The focus then moves to a more overt account of his feelings of dread: 'a weight at my heart and a feeling of impending danger'…
5–6	You have clearly explained the effects of the choice of language. You have used a range of relevant quotations. You have used subject terminology appropriately.	The passage looks like part of a diary. He starts with a short sentence and follows it with a long, descriptive sentence about the landscape. This sets a mood of 'melancholy', which is his mood. He feels the 'weight' of fear and responsibility and analyses why he feels like this, answering a rhetorical question: 'Have I not cause for such a feeling?'

Page 16: Analysing Form and Structure

1. Up to **[2]** for any reasonable answer to each question up to a maximum of **[10]**.
  a) A boarding house / in a city / a place where single people rent rooms / Second Avenue (New York / America).
  b) 'Small and unobtrusive' / dressed plainly / shy / does not draw attention to herself / not interested in what's going on.
  c) Does not fit with the previous description of her / a change in mood / shows an interest in Andy / shows that she is sharp or intelligent / suggests she is judging him.
  d) He is polite or well-mannered / he has charm / he is starting a successful career / he is shallow or superficial / he is not interested in Miss Conway.
  e) She does something to make herself noticed / they get to know each other / they fall in love / they argue / it turns out that they know each other / any other reasonable conjecture.

2. a–y, b–z, c–x

[1] for each up to a maximum of **[3]**

English Language 1 – pages 17–20

Page 17: Creative Reading 1

1.

A naive/unreliable narrator	A
An omniscient narrator	D
A reliable first-person narrator	B
An intrusive narrator	C (also omniscient)

[2] for each up to a maximum of **[8]**

Page 18: Creative Reading 2

[1] for each correct answer in 'How we learn' and up to **[2]** for a reasonable explanation in 'What we learn' up to a maximum of **[15]**.

1.

Character	How we learn about the character	What we learn
Hyde's housekeeper:	a)	She is a bad person / she cannot be trusted / she is polite.
Magwitch:	b)	He is aggressive / rough / frightening.
Darcy:	e)	People are generally impressed by him when they first meet him but quickly change their minds because of the way he behaves.
Mrs Reed:	d)	She is bad-tempered / aggressive / cruel / uncaring.
Victor Frankenstein:	c)	He is behaving strangely / he is sick / he is hysterical. He worries his friend.

Page 19: Narrative Writing

The following answers are examples of the sort of thing you might write. Your own answers will be completely different.
[1] for each reasonable answer.

1. **a)** First person; yes. **b)** Formal, using Standard English.
    c) Female; 82; Small, neat, well-dressed; Grew up on a farm and married a farmer, now living in a bungalow in a village; A widow, with two children who live abroad, friendly with the neighbours but no close friends; Speaks in a Cornish accent but uses Standard English. **[maximum 8]**
2. **a)** In the village post office. **b)** Yes, she goes abroad.
    c) Now. **d)** A year. **e)** Yes (except for some memories in flashback). **[maximum 5]**
3. Exposition: Doris leads a quiet life in a small village with her two cats. Inciting incident: She wins the lottery. She decides to visit her children but not tell them she's a millionaire. Turning point: She goes to see her daughter in France, who is too busy to be bothered. She books her a ticket to Australia. In Australia her son lets her stay but after a while he puts her in a horrible home. Climax: She buys the nursing home, improves the lives of its patients and returns home, where she spends the rest of her money on herself and on charities. Coda/ending: Doris is living happily in the village with her cats and a man she met in the nursing home. She has spent all her money and not given any to her children. **[maximum 5]**

Page 20: Descriptive Writing

The following answers are examples of the sort of thing you might write. Your own answers will be completely different. **[1]** for each reasonable answer up to a maximum of **[20]** overall.

1. **a)** Third.
    b) Past.
2. **a)** Gaudy rides, milling crowds.
    b) Screeching child, loud dance music.
    c) Spicy sausage, burning wood.
    d) Tangy mustard, sweet toffee.
    e) Sticky candyfloss, slimy mud.
3. **a)** A blur of swirling colours and harsh noises.
    b) Candy-striped stall; fluffy toys piled high.
    c) Blue nylon fur, plastic brown eyes.
4. **a)** The crowd rumbled and rolled like a storm-tossed ship.
    b) An explosion of excited laughter.

English Language 2 – pages 21–22

Page 21: Reading Non-fiction 1 and 2

1. Up to **[2]** for each answer similar to the following up to a maximum of **[20]**:

	Text A	Text B
What is the writer's attitude to Little Mickledon?	Likes it. Finds it 'charming and tranquil'.	Does not like the peace and quiet: 'totally cut off'.
What is the writer's opinion of the B & B?	Finds it 'delightful' and gives positive impression of the owners.	Finds it a 'disappointment', criticizes several aspects and does not like owners' attitude.
What impression do you get of the writer?	Someone who likes peace and quiet. Someone who focuses on positive aspects.	Someone who likes to be in touch. Someone who likes to criticize / likes to find fault.
How would you describe the general tone and style?	Positive/enthusiastic/vague	Negative/critical/honest
Comment on language features.	Uses words like 'relax', 'calm' and 'tranquil' to give an impression of peace and quiet. Uses archaic words/spellings (Olde, yore) and puts quotation marks round 'civilization'.	Colloquial – addresses readers with imperative ('Be warned'). Uses adjectives to give an unflattering picture: 'grubby', 'pitiful', 'hippy'.

Page 22: Writing Non-fiction 1 and 2

1. The following are only suggestions. There are many other points you could make. **[1]** for each up to a maximum of **[10]**.

Pros	Cons
Studying for exams is much more important.	It helps you understand the importance of things like punctuality and politeness.
The work being done is not interesting or meaningful.	It helps you choose your future career.
Students on work experience are just free labour.	You can learn new skills.
In the time you cannot get a realistic idea of what the work is like.	You might make contacts which would lead to paid employment.
You've got the rest of your life to experience work.	You get to meet a wide range of people.

2. **[1]** for each of the following up to a maximum of **[5]**:
   - opening with 'Dear Sir' or 'Dear Editor'
   - setting out the opening correctly
   - using a formal tone
   - clearly stating the purpose of your letter
   - putting your point of view strongly and clearly
   - using a rhetorical or literary device
   - accurate spelling and punctuation.
3. **[1]** for each of the following up to a maximum of **[5]**:
   - using an intriguing/amusing headline
   - using a strapline
   - using an appropriate informal tone
   - clearly stating the purpose of your article
   - putting your point of view strongly and clearly
   - using a rhetorical or literary device
   - accurate spelling and punctuation.

Shakespeare – pages 23–24

Page 23: Context and Themes
1. Up to **[2]** for each reasonable answer up to a maximum of **[12]**.
2. Up to **[2]** for each reasonable answer up to a maximum of **[12]**.

Page 24: Characters, Language and Structure
1. **[2]** for each quotation and **[2]** for a reasonable interpretation up to a maximum of **[12]**.
2. **[1]** for each correct answer and up to **[2]** for a reasonable explanation similar to the suggestions below up to a maximum of **[12]**.
   a) Oxymoron. Its use suggests confusion about love and how the themes of love and hate are intertwined in the play. **b)** Metaphor. The speaker (Shylock) picks up on an insulting comparison and extends it to warn that he can 'bite.' **c)** Rhetorical question. The speaker (Cassius) is trying to get Brutus to think about whether Caesar's name should be synonymous with power and so questions his power. **d)** Pathetic fallacy / personification. The speaker claims that the wind and thunder have told him about Prospero, reflecting his own fear as well as Prospero's power.

The Nineteenth-Century Novel – pages 25–26

Page 25: Context and Themes
1. Up to **[2]** for each reasonable answer up to a maximum of **[10]**.
2. **a)** **[1]** for each reasonable answer up to a maximum of **[5]**.
   b) Up to **[2]** for each reasonable answer up to a maximum of **[10]**.

Page 26: Characters, Language and Structure
1. **[1]** for every box completed with a reasonable answer up to a maximum of **[25]**.
2. a–x, b–v, c–y, d–z, e–w
   [2] for each correct answer up to a maximum of **[10]**

Modern Texts – pages 27–28

Page 27: Context and Themes
Below are examples of the kind of answer you might have given. Up to **[5]** for each reasonable answer similar to these, depending on how full your answer is.
1. **a)** *An Inspector Calls* is set shortly before the First World War, in 1912, in a 'large city' in the Midlands. The family is middle-class and wealthy, Mr Birling being a self-made man who has married someone from a higher social class. They are 'comfortable' and smug but the Inspector reveals the dark underside of their world.
   b) The world of *Never Let Me Go* seems to be just like the real world of just a few years ago. However, there are aspects of this world which are not real (as far as we know). Breeding people to provide spare parts is not something that is done officially now, although there are cases of people having children to provide genetic material for existing children who are sick.
   c) *DNA* was written as part of a national scheme to produce new plays for schools and youth groups. The writer states that the names and even genders of the characters can be changed to suit the group performing the play. Some might say this leads to a lack of definition in many of the characters.
2. **a)** **[1]** for each theme up to a maximum of **[4]**.
   b) Up to **[2]** for each reasonable answer up to a maximum of **[8]**.

Page 28: Characters, Language and Structure
1. **[1]** for every box completed with a reasonable answer up to a maximum of **[25]**.
2. **[1]** for each reasonable answer up to a maximum of **[10]**.

Poetry – pages 29–32

Page 29: Context and Themes
1. **a)** 'Follower' **[1]** **b)** 'Singh Song!' **[1]** **c)** Sonnet 29 ('I think of thee!') **[1]**
2. **a)** Extract from 'The Prelude' **[1]** **b)** 'Kamikaze' **[1]**
   c) 'Remains' **[1]**
   For questions 3 and 4, the following answers are suggestions. You may have listed other poems. **[1]** for each title listed appropriately, up to a maximum of **[12]**.
3. **a)** 'Before You Were Mine'; 'Eden Rock'; 'Follower'; 'Walking Away'; 'Mother, any distance'. **b)** 'When We Two Parted'; 'Neutral Tones'; 'Porphyria's Lover'; 'The Farmer's Bride'.
   c) 'Follower'; 'Singh Song!'; 'Before You Were Mine'; 'Letters from Yorkshire'. **d)** 'Love's Philosophy'; Sonnet 29; 'Winter Swans'; 'Singh Song!'
4. **a)** 'The Charge of the Light Brigade'; 'Exposure'; 'Bayonet Charge'; 'Remains'. **b)** 'Poppies'; 'War Photographer'; 'The Émigrée'; 'Kamikaze'. **c)** 'London'; 'My Last Duchess'; 'Checking Out Me History'; 'The Charge of the Light Brigade'.
   d) Extract from 'The Prelude'; 'Checking Out Me History'; 'Poppies'; 'The Émigrée'.

Page 30: Language, Form and Structure
1. **[1]** for each technique identified and **[1]** for each reasonable explanation (the explanations below are suggestions only), up to a maximum of **[40]**.
   a) Alliteration, pathetic fallacy. The alliteration of 'l' and 's' (also called sibilance) helps to make the line sound gentle and sad. The image of the earth starving adds to the sense of bleakness and despair. **[4]**
   b) Repetition, archaic language. The repetition of 'long' increases our sense of the future stretching ahead. The archaic language perhaps makes it sound more important. **[4]**
   c) Pathetic fallacy, onomatopoeia, enjambment. The image of the earth gulping for breath suggests the mood of the poet at the beginning of the poem. 'Gulping' might reflect the sound of the muddy earth beneath his feet. The enjambment reflects the continuity of movement and mood. **[6]**
   d) Caesura, metaphor. The caesuras might give a sense of separation, as well as giving emphasis to the two single-word sentences that follow. The two metaphors give us a picture of the poet and his mother's roles in the relationship. He is flying away and she is holding him to the ground. **[4]**
   e) Dialect, rhyming couplet, enjambment. The use of dialect gives a sense of the speaker's heritage and identity. The rhyming couplet gives the poem a light-hearted tone in contrast with its serious subject

matter, as well as reflecting the childish or simple nature of what he was told. The enjambment also makes the lines seem childish, as the poet uses 'and' to build a list. **[6]**

f) Assonance, simile, end-stopping. The repetition of the long 'o' adds to a sense of calm. Comparing the darkroom to the church makes the photographer's work seem spiritual and important. The end-stop makes us pause, almost as if pausing before entering the church-like room. **[6]**

g) Enjambment, caesura, simile, onomatopoeia/alliteration. The enjambment gives a sense of the continuous nature of one aspect of the storm, while the caesura reflects how it can suddenly stop and start again. The simile is almost an oxymoron, as 'spit' and 'tame' do not seem to go together. Perhaps the poet is implying that cats are never really tame and, similarly, the storm cannot be tamed. 'Spit' and 'spray' could be seen as onomatopoeia, the 'sp' sounds reflecting the noise made by the water. **[10]**

Page 31: Unseen Poetry

1. Up to **[2]** for each answer similar to those below. Other answers might be equally valid.
   a) It is set in a forest during a storm.
   b) No, it is irregular (free verse). The lack of regular patterns reflects the unpredictability of the storm.

c) 'Cackle with uncouth sounds' conveys the harshness of the sounds described. It could be called onomatopoeia.
d) In 'white liquid fire, bright white' the short 'i's are sharp and quick, like the lightning.
e) Describing the lightning as a 'white snake' adds a sense of danger as well as painting a vivid picture.
f) By adding a lot of details in this simple way, the poet builds a sense of the way the storm continues and shows no sign of stopping.
g) The repetition of this phrase and the shortness of the line give it greater impact, emphasizing that humans may think they have harnessed the power of electricity but they cannot really tame nature.
h) The power and wonder of nature – the insignificance of humans – the arrogance of humans.
i) He is in awe of nature – he is excited and perhaps frightened by the storm – it makes him feel insignificant – it makes him realize that humans are not really powerful.
j) Any answer rooted in the text. **[maximum 20]**

Page 32: Unseen Poetry

2. The answers below are suggestions. There may be other valid responses. Up to **[2]** for every box filled in with a reasonable response, up to a maximum of **[32]**.

	'Storm in the Black Forest'	'The Vixen'
Setting (time and place)	In a forest during a storm.	The poem takes place in the woods on what seems to be a typical day for the vixen.
What happens in the poem	The poet describes the stages of a violent storm and how it never seems to end, making him think about man and nature.	The poet describes the behaviour of a vixen and her cubs, and how she reacts to danger.
Structure	Four stanzas of unequal lengths (one of only one line) and lines of different lengths, giving a sense of unpredictability.	One stanza of 14 lines, describing what happens in a controlled way. 14 lines, as in a sonnet, but not sonnet structure.
Rhythm and rhyme	No regularity – again reflecting the storm.	Iambic pentameter – smooth and regular. Rhyming couplets – simple structure, each couplet describing one small action.
Vocabulary/register	Language of richness (bronzey), danger (snake), movement (wriggling) and science (electric) combine to convey awe and wonder.	Everyday, straightforward language.
Use of sound	Alliteration and assonance used to suggest the sounds of the storm.	Sounds made by vixen conveyed by onomatopoeia. Alliteration in line 13.
Imagery	Metaphor and personification used to give vivid impression of the power of the storm.	Literal imagery: the poem describes the scene.
Themes and the poet's attitude	The power of nature; the arrogance of man; the wonder of nature. The last stanza draws a 'lesson' from the experience. He is excited and frightened by nature and impressed by its power. He feels humans are comparatively powerless, though they think they are powerful.	Tension between nature and man; motherhood; the beauty of nature. He is impressed by the vixen's care for her cubs. He sees the danger posed by humans from her point of view. The ending gives a positive, hopeful view of life.

Practice Exam Papers – pages 33–56

Page 34 English Language Paper 1 – Section A: Reading

1. Any four from:
   - mirrors
   - cakes
   - sweetmeats
   - chocolates
   - wedding cake.

   [1] for each up to a maximum of [4]

2. Look at the mark scheme below, decide which description is closest to your answer and then decide what mark to give it up to a maximum of [8].

Marks	Skills	Examples of possible content
7–8	You have analysed the effects of the choice of language. You have used an appropriate range of quotations. You have used sophisticated subject terminology appropriately.	The first sentence, although quite long, is a simple sentence and does not make the shop sound especially attractive. The simile 'like the butt of a cigar' is not appealing, being something thrown away, and not appropriate for children. The writer seems to realize this when he says 'One should rather say', as if correcting himself, and his new simile 'like the butt of a firework' is better. You can imagine children gathering round the butt of a firework and looking at the colours. This leads into a detailed description of the contents of the window, focusing on the bright colours…
5–6	You have clearly explained the effects of the choice of language. You have used a range of relevant quotations. You have used subject terminology appropriately.	He uses long sentences to list all the sweets and chocolates, putting across their attraction by using imagery. It glows 'like the butt of a firework', which is something children would like. He makes it seem alive by saying the light is 'dancing'. The sweets seem unobtainable to the children, whose noses are 'glued' to the window but do not go in. They are called 'gutter-snipes' so are probably poor, in contrast with the richness of the shop window.

3. Look at the mark scheme below, decide which description is closest to your answer and then decide which mark to give yourself up to a maximum of [8].

Marks	Skills	Examples of possible content
7–8	You have analysed the use of structural features. You have chosen an appropriate range of examples. You have used a range of subject terminology accurately.	The description of the shop window in the first paragraph makes an ordinary setting seem enticing and almost exotic. Introducing the 'gutter-snipes' makes us think of people wanting something they cannot have, so when the focus moves to Angus, we have a sense of his wanting something too. The second paragraph gives his background, establishing something about his character and what he does. In the third paragraph, another character is introduced as he moves into the shop…
5–6	You have clearly explained the effect of structural features. You have chosen relevant examples. You have used subject terminology accurately.	At first the focus is on the shop window, giving a sense of how attractive it is to children. When it moves from the children to the young man we wonder what the attraction is for him. After we learn about him, we find out. The third paragraph describes the attractive young waitress. In the final paragraph he places his order and, after a pause, suddenly asks her to marry him, leaving the reader wondering about their relationship.

4. Look at the mark scheme below, decide which description is closest to your answer and then decide which mark to give yourself up to a maximum of **[20]**.

Marks	Skills	Examples of possible content
16–20	You have critically evaluated the text in a detailed way. You have used examples from the text to explain your views convincingly. You have analysed a range of the writer's methods. You have used a range of relevant quotations to support your views.	The writer introduces Angus by describing him looking into the shop window with the children, thus associating him with the children. He too wants something that maybe he cannot have, something that has a 'fiery charm' for him. The description of the wedding cake, 'remote and satisfying', is a clue about what this is. In the second paragraph, the description of his appearance and background makes him sound eccentric and full of contradictions. He is 'listless' and 'resolute' at the same time. He has been disinherited by a rich uncle apparently for being against Socialism, whereas you might expect the opposite. His actions in the shop are just as eccentric.
11–15	You have clearly evaluated the text. You have used examples from the text to explain your views clearly. You have clearly explained the effect of the writer's methods. You have used some relevant quotations to support your views.	The description of Angus gives odd details, such as that he was 'disinherited for Socialism' by his rich uncle. The writer builds up a clear picture of what he looks like, as he does with the young lady. At first it seems as if their relationship is just that between a waitress and a regular customer as he passes her 'merely raising his hat' and then just orders a bun. However, when he proposes to her, as if he is ordering something else, the reader wants to know more about them.

Page 35 English Language Paper 1 – Section B: Writing

5. Look at the mark scheme below, decide which description is closest to your answer and then decide which mark to give yourself. This task is marked for content and organization, and for technical accuracy.
   Content and Organization [maximum 24]

22–24	**Content** You have communicated convincingly and compellingly throughout. Your tone, style and register assuredly match purpose, form and audience. You have used an extensive and ambitious vocabulary with sustained crafting of linguistic devices. **Organization** Your writing is highly structured and developed, including a range of integrated and complex ideas. Your paragraphs are fluently linked with integrated discourse markers. You have used a variety of structural features in an inventive way.
19–21	**Content** You have communicated convincingly. Your tone, style and register consistently match purpose, form and audience. You have used an extensive vocabulary with evidence of conscious crafting of linguistic devices. **Organization** Your writing is structured and developed, including a range of engaging and complex ideas. You have used paragraphs consistently with integrated discourse markers. You have used a variety of structural features effectively.

Technical Accuracy [maximum 16]

13–16	You have consistently demarcated sentences accurately. You have used a wide range of punctuation with a high level of accuracy. You have used a full range of sentence forms for effect. You have used Standard English consistently and accurately, with secure control of grammatical structures. You have achieved a high level of accuracy in spelling, including ambitious vocabulary. Your use of vocabulary is extensive and ambitious.
9–12	You have usually demarcated sentences accurately. You have used a range of punctuation, usually accurately. You have used a variety of sentence forms for effect. You have used Standard English appropriately, with control of grammatical structures. You have spelled most words, including complex and irregular words, correctly. Your use of vocabulary is increasingly sophisticated.

[maximum 40]

Page 38 English Language Paper 2 – Section A: Reading

1. A, B, F, H [maximum 4]
2. Look at the mark scheme below, decide which description is closest to your answer and then decide what mark to give it up to a maximum of [8].

Marks	Skills	Examples of possible content
7–8	You have given a perceptive interpretation of both texts. You have synthesized evidence from the texts. You have used appropriate quotations from both texts.	In 1891 the libraries in Marylebone are new, although the buildings they are in are unsuitable, one being 'plain and insufficient', contrasting with the King's Park library, which was built over 100 years ago but is 'roomy' and 'generously proportioned'. The number of people using this library is falling, reflecting the fact that the area is not 'thriving', while in Marylebone, where the libraries are 'in two of the most populous parts of the parish', 'the demand increases daily'.
5–6	You have started to interpret both texts. You have shown clear connections between texts. You have used relevant quotations from both texts.	The libraries in Marylebone are not funded by the council. King's Park is run by the council but the council does not want it and says it is not attracting enough people. They also say it is only really pensioners who use it, whereas the Marylebone libraries are used by 'persons of all sorts and conditions'. In Marylebone the buildings are cramped and unattractive but the King's Park library is 'roomy' and 'beautifully decorated'.

3. Look at the mark scheme below, decide which description is closest to your answer and then decide which mark to give it up to a maximum of [12].

Marks	Skills	Examples of possible content
10–12	You have analysed the effects of the choice of language.You have used an appropriate range of quotations. You have used sophisticated subject terminology appropriately.	The tone is extremely polite and to a modern reader might even seem sycophantic, the writer's signing off with 'We beg, Sir, to remain yours obediently'. It seems odd that they would be 'obedient' to a newspaper editor but it must have been the convention of the time, as it reflects the courteous tone of the whole letter (for example, the use of modal verbs: 'May we be allowed'; 'We would'). The use of long, complex sentences also makes the tone seem reasonable and polite…
7–9	You have clearly explained the effects of the choice of language. You have used a range of relevant quotations. You have used subject terminology appropriately.	The tone is very gentle. They start with a question, which explains what they want in a very polite way. In the second paragraph they say what they are not going to do, giving the idea that people already agree with them. They give a long explanation, in the past tense, of the history of their libraries. They use statistics as evidence to impress the reader with their 'success', a word they keep repeating.

Page 39

4. Look at the mark scheme below, decide which description is closest to your answer and then decide which mark to give it up to a maximum of **[16]**.

Marks	Skills	Examples of possible content
13–16	You have compared ideas and perspectives in a perceptive way. You have analysed methods used to convey ideas and perspectives. You have used a range of appropriate quotations.	The two sources have different purposes. A's is to report on the campaign to save the library and B's is to persuade people to support public libraries. However, A includes both direct and reported speech from several people who are trying to keep the library open and who use emotive language, such as 'heart' and 'devastating', together with personal anecdotes, clichés ('drop in the ocean') and rhetorical techniques such as rhetorical questions ('how can the Mayor…?') to persuade. Source B also uses rhetorical techniques but is more subtle. The letter starts by saying what it is NOT going to do, implying confidence that the argument for public libraries has been won. Its tone is calm and measured, its arguments backed by evidence. This is similar to the way the council spokesperson in source A puts her case…
9–12	You have compared ideas and perspectives in a clear and relevant way. You have explained clearly methods used to convey ideas and perspectives. You have used relevant quotations from both texts.	Witherspoon is reporting the views of others while Debenham and Hollond give their own point of view. More people who are against the library closure are quoted than people who are in favour, so in the article you get a stronger impression of their point of view. They all use emotive language. The council's response seems cold and uncaring, focusing on 'statistics'. The letter is very unemotional and uses logical arguments and facts and figures to argue for public libraries – a bit like the council's arguments in Source A.

Page 39 English Language Paper 2 – Section B: Writing

5. Look at the mark scheme for page 35 question 5 above, decide which description is closest to your answer and then decide which mark to give yourself up to a maximum of **[40]**. This task is marked for content and organization, and for technical accuracy.

Page 41 English Literature Paper 1 – Shakespeare and the Nineteenth-Century Novel
Section A: Shakespeare

For all questions, look at the mark scheme below, decide which description is closest to your answer and then decide which mark to give yourself up to a maximum of **[30]**.

Marks	Skills
26–30	You have responded to the task in an exploratory and critical way. You have used precise, appropriate references to support your interpretation. You have analysed the writer's methods using subject terminology appropriately. You have explored the effects of the writer's methods. You have explored links between text and ideas/context.
21–25	You have responded to the task in a thoughtful, developed way. You have used appropriate references to support your interpretation. You have examined the writer's methods using subject terminology effectively. You have examined the effects of the writer's methods. You have thoughtfully considered links between text and ideas/context.

This question is also marked for AO4 (spelling, punctuation and grammar) up to a maximum of **[4]**.

Marks	Description of performance
4	You have spelled and punctuated with consistent accuracy. You have consistently used vocabulary and sentence structures to achieve effective control of meaning.
2–3	You have spelled and punctuated with considerable accuracy. You have consistently used a considerable range of vocabulary and sentence structures to achieve general control of meaning.

Your answers could include some of the following points.
1. *Macbeth*
   - Macbeth is seen here preparing for battle; he is a soldier again.
   - Speaking in soliloquy, he says he has no fear.
   - He is aware of what he has done.
   - Ambiguity in 'she should have died hereafter'.
   - Repetition of 'tomorrow' and imagery used to describe time.
   - Imagery conveys one man's insignificance and the pointlessness of life.
   - Macbeth as a brave commander at the start of the play.
   - Influence of the witches and Lady Macbeth.
   - His conscience and feelings of guilt.

- His murders, cruelty and tyranny.
- His heroic defiance and bravery at the end of the play.

2. *Romeo and Juliet*
   - Juliet's desire for Romeo to stay, pretending it is still night.
   - Imagery of light and dark – they can only be together in the dark.
   - The marriage is consummated and so is a real marriage – important later in the play.
   - Romeo's use of nature imagery/personification.
   - Imagery reflects the enormity of their passion.
   - Awareness of danger – love and death.
   - Earlier, Juliet insisted on marriage as proof of Romeo's love.
   - Marriage seen as political tool by Capulet.
   - Marriages arranged by parents.
   - Marriage as holy – spiritual and sexual fulfilment.
   - Nurse's disregard for the sanctity of marriage as well as for Juliet's feelings.

Page 42

3. *The Tempest*
   - Powerful images of spirits chasing the men.
   - Comic version of revenge – the plot to kill Prospero as a comic sub-plot.
   - Prospero using magic, as he does to capture and control those who took his kingdom.
   - Language used to describe torture, including alliteration, conveys delight in inflicting pain.
   - Audience left wondering what Prospero will do with the others who are at his mercy.
   - For most of the play Prospero seems intent on revenge.
   - Caliban seeks revenge on Prospero.
   - The last act shows Prospero choosing to forgive.
   - Forgiveness and reconciliation more powerful and more satisfying than revenge.

Page 43

4. *The Merchant of Venice*
   - He sees Antonio as a 'fool' for lending without interest, recalling that moneylenders had to be outsiders.
   - He has no interest in appearing merciful as society might expect.
   - Repetition of 'my bond' shows anger.
   - He recalls his former treatment by Antonio.
   - Calling him a dog implies Jews are seen as less than human.
   - The jailer has allowed Antonio to 'come abroad' – Antonio, the insider, is not seen as a criminal.
   - His description of how he will not behave implies that such behaviour is expected from him towards Christians. He is rebelling against this.
   - Antonio's earlier treatment of him showed that anti-Semitism is the norm.
   - Scenes with Jessica and his servants show how Jewish society is separate and different from the rest of Venice.

5. *Much Ado About Nothing*
   - Benedick has not yet appeared, but we anticipate a clash and/or romance with Beatrice.
   - Beatrice asks if he is with Don Pedro, indicating an interest in him.
   - Something happened the last time they met but we never know exactly what.
   - Contrast between the messenger's account of Benedick as a 'good soldier' and Beatrice's.
   - She does not seem to want to hear anything good about him.
   - Leonato's reference to a 'merry war' makes us expect battles of wits – but is there real dislike or is it all a joke?
   - They argue and misunderstand each other but their friends think they are suited.
   - Compare/contrast their relationship with the more conventional wooing of Hero by Claudio.
   - Their reactions to Claudio's treatment of Hero.

Page 44

6. *Julius Caesar*
   - Brutus's love for Portia shows a strong marriage.
   - Portia argues that love requires trust.
   - She feels she has been 'left out' of the conspiracy because of her sex.
   - She has to 'prove' she is as brave and trustworthy as a man.
   - Her way of proving it (taken from Shakespeare's sources) is shocking to Elizabethan and modern audiences but was thought admirable by Romans.
   - She defines herself by her father's reputation. She sees herself as better than other women.
   - Compare/contrast with Calpurnia, Caesar's wife.
   - Her suicide – seen as honourable in the context of ancient Rome.

Page 45 English Literature Paper 1 – Shakespeare and the Nineteenth-Century Novel.

Section B: The Nineteenth-Century Novel

See mark scheme above for Section A. This question does not carry additional marks for spelling, punctuation and grammar. Your answers could include some of the following points.

7. *The Strange Case of Dr Jekyll and Mr Hyde*
   - The story is told by Poole, introducing another narrator.
   - Another piece of the jigsaw for Utterson and the reader.
   - Poole very close to Jekyll but is convinced it is not Jekyll.
   - Poole's reaction one of fear, his hair standing up – feels he has seen something evil.
   - Compares the man he saw to a rat – Hyde is often compared to animals. He is also referred to as 'it', as if he is no longer human.
   - Jekyll has physically shrunk – 'more of a dwarf' – matching other descriptions of Hyde.
   - Stevenson is building up gradually to a full description of transformation.
   - Utterson and others assume Hyde is a separate person. They see Jekyll as 'good'.
   - Consider Dr Lanyon's narrative and his reaction.
   - Consider Jekyll's own narrative and his motivation – to separate good and evil.
   - The story shows that this is impossible – what else does it say about good and evil?

8. *A Christmas Carol*
   - Here Dickens uses shock and horror, surprising the reader at the end of the chapter.
   - The two children are personifications of Ignorance and Want (poverty).
   - The language used to describe them is vivid and repulsive.
   - However, the description is not very much exaggerated – it is what very poor children would look like.
   - The ghost uses them as a warning of what might happen if poverty and lack of education are not dealt with – revolution.
   - Dickens uses Scrooge's transformation to explore ideas about responsibility.
   - Using the Christmas ghost story, a popular form, Dickens gets his messages across in an entertaining way.
   - Being charitable and socially responsible is part of the spirit of Christmas – it does not stop you enjoying yourself.
   - This chapter shows a wide range of people at Christmas, many poor.
   - The Cratchits are used to show what life is like for poor families and how easy it could be to improve their lives.

Page 46

9. *Great Expectations*
   - The voice is that of the adult Pip looking back on his childhood.
   - He makes us aware of the child's innocence and naivety, realizing for the first time that his parents are really dead.

- There is some irony in the adult narrator's description of the child's fear.
- Pip recreates his feelings as a child – a mixture of comedy (the church being upside-down) and terror.
- His descriptions of the landscape, creating atmosphere and setting the tone.
- For most of the novel we, like Pip, are kept in ignorance about Magwitch.
- The reader empathizes with Pip but can see that he makes poor judgements.
- The novel as a 'Bildungsroman' – the story of Pip's education in life.

10. *Jane Eyre*
- As narrator Jane shares the feelings she had at the time with the reader.
- Here she analyses her feelings, which she does throughout the novel.
- She opens with a rhetorical question and answers it.
- She analyses Rochester's character, calling him 'proud, sardonic, harsh' but also listing his good qualities.
- She is concerned with morality. It is important for her to think he is no longer immoral.
- It is now clear that she is in love with him, a feeling that has been developing throughout the novel.
- Jane rescues Rochester on several occasions – almost as if he has to be less powerful for her to love him.
- Symbolism of the fire and Rochester's attitude to Jane after it.
- His marriage to Bertha and his deception – Jane's reasons for leaving Thornfield.
- Jane's return to Thornfield and their mutual love.

Page 47

11. *Frankenstein*
- Physical description of Elizabeth's 'loveliness'.
- This is followed by a description of her nature, painting her as an ideal woman.
- Frankenstein in love with her – has she any other purpose in the novel?
- The other woman mentioned, Justine, is also seen as good, innocent and an object of love.
- Neither Elizabeth nor Justine has any real power, relying on men to help them.
- They are both innocent victims of Frankenstein and his creature.
- Female characters are secondary in the novel and do not take an active role.
- However, they are almost always seen as good and pure.
- Consider how this reflects female roles in the Gothic tradition and in early nineteenth-century society.

12. *Pride and Prejudice*
- Contrast in reactions of Mr and Mrs Bennet.
- Elizabeth's reasons for rejecting Mr Collins.
- Ironic/comic tone of passage.
- Use of dialogue to convey attitudes of Mr and Mrs Bennet and their characters.
- Serious point given to unlikely character to make in a comic way. Who will maintain her if she is not married?
- Contrast Elizabeth's refusal with Charlotte Lucas's acceptance of Mr Collins.
- Marriage must be for love but must also make sense financially and socially.
- Other examples of marriage: Mr and Mrs Bennet, Lydia and Wickham, Jane and Bingley.
- Marriage of Elizabeth and Darcy as an ideal.

Page 48

13. *The Sign of Four*
- The mysterious atmosphere created by description of the moonlit night.
- Passage focuses on the discovery of the body, which changes the investigation to a murder case.

- Description of body brings home reality of violent death.
- Language used to describe the scene and Watson's reaction creates sense of horror.
- Detailed description of room sets up murder as a puzzle.
- The note introduces the mystery of the 'sign of four'.
- Novel explores the effect of murder on people and society.
- Explores what makes people murder.
- Murder gives Holmes a chance to demonstrate his skills.
- Consider the conventions of the detective story.

Page 50 English Literature Paper 2 – Modern Texts and Poetry. Section A: Modern Prose or Drama

Use the mark scheme for English Literature Paper 1 (above). This question is also marked on your spelling, punctuation and grammar (maximum **[34]** in all).
Your answers could include some of the following points.

1. *An Inspector Calls*
- Eva Smith as a representative of the working class.
- Is she one person or several people?
- The inspector shows the photo to the Birlings separately.
- She is involved with all the Birlings.
- The situations she is in are almost stereotypical.
- The Birlings' treatment of her reveals their characters and attitudes.

2. *An Inspector Calls*
- The Birlings and their house are comfortable and middle-class – they are smug.
- Their main concern is making and spending money.
- Mr Birling is not concerned about his workers or their lives.
- Mrs Birling does charity work but does not appear to really care.
- The children are only interested in spending money.
- They cannot see what Eva has to do with them.
- To different degrees they are made to see how selfish they are.
- Refer to the Inspector's speech about responsibility.

3. *Blood Brothers*
- The fact of their being brothers demonstrates the importance of class in their futures.
- They behave and speak differently.
- Edward has opportunities that Mickey does not have.
- Is it just money or is there more to class?
- There does not seem to be any social mobility in the play.
- The differences between them are quite crudely drawn.
- The two boys are not different in nature – their differences are the result of upbringing.

4. *Blood Brothers*
- The opening immediately tells us the deaths are inevitable.
- Mrs Johnstone is very superstitious. Mrs Lyons mocks at first but changes.
- The narrator often refers to superstitions.
- The idea that events are pre-ordained has more to do with social class than fate.
- What happens is the result of choices characters have made.
- Do they refer to fate and superstitions as a way of avoiding responsibility?

5. *The History Boys*
- The character of the charismatic unconventional teacher is common in fiction.
- Bennett, through other characters, shows an awareness of this.
- He does not belong in the modern world of school (even in the 1980s).
- He is a complex character as a teacher – inspirational and fun but with ambivalent attitudes to the value of education.
- He is witty and can be incisive but sometimes is just saying things to be clever.
- Compare/contrast with personalities and styles of other teachers in the play.
- His 'groping' and the reactions to it – the tolerant attitude towards it is not what we would expect today. Is it realistic?

6. *The History Boys*
   - Why has Bennett made the choice to have all the boys studying history (unlikely in real life)?
   - Is it just a way of passing exams?
   - Mrs Lintott and Irwin have different approaches. Irwin wants to question everything.
   - Is this any better than accepting everything?
   - The idea that there is 'no need to tell the truth'.
   - Irwin's subsequent career involves him in making history.

Page 51

7. *DNA*
   - The other teenagers physically abuse Adam.
   - There is psychological bullying in the group. John Tate bullies to keep power.
   - Phil's treatment of Leah could be seen as bullying.
   - When John Tate gives up he is seen as weak.
   - What is meant by 'bullying'? How are possible meanings reflected in the play?
   - What is the difference between bullying and leadership?

8. *DNA*
   - He only appears briefly but has a central role.
   - He tries to control the others through fear.
   - He threatens and patronizes others.
   - He tries to ban the word 'dead'. Why?
   - He loses control as things get serious.
   - The reports of him 'losing it' later suggest he feels guilt.
   - Compare/contrast with Cathy, who is truly ruthless.

9. *The Curious Incident of the Dog in the Night-Time*
   - Christopher accepts his father's version of events, as does the audience at first.
   - His desire to solve the mystery leads him to the truth.
   - Judy speaks through letters.
   - Her version of events is very different.
   - She gives the other side of living with Christopher, admitting she could not cope.
   - She presents a nostalgic view of family life.
   - In the end she returns and commits to Christopher.

10. *The Curious Incident of the Dog in the Night-Time*
    - Christopher is in a Special Needs school.
    - It is not spelled out in the text but he appears to have been diagnosed with autism.
    - We do not see him interact with other pupils but his stories show he thinks they are stupid.
    - He is extremely good at Maths and is entered for exams.
    - His relationship with Siobhan is crucial.
    - It is not clear what (if any) benefit Christopher gets from his education.
    - It does not go into issues around autism / special needs / education. The situation is accepted as it is.

11. *A Taste of Honey*
    - The mother–daughter relationship is central.
    - She argues with her mother about everything and resents their way of life.
    - She knows nothing about her father and is worried by what her mother tells her about him.
    - There is a role-reversal, Jo seemingly more mature than Helen.
    - Jo is critical of her mother but puts up with her.
    - Jo is motivated by not wanting to be like her mother.
    - She feels she can do without her but in the end has no-one else.

12. *A Taste of Honey*
    - Helen is an irresponsible parent.
    - Jo appears more responsible but does not always think about consequences.
    - The boy disappears after getting Jo pregnant – he takes no responsibility.
    - Jo's father did not take responsibility for her; Helen implies he was incapable of doing so.
    - Jo matures by facing up to her responsibility for the baby.
    - Geoff steps in when Helen has left but goes when she returns. Is he serious about looking after Jo?

- When Helen returns she seems to be willing to help but changes when she learns the baby's father is black. Will she return?

Page 52

13. *Lord of the Flies*
    - Ralph is typically British, according to the conventions of the time.
    - He would not be out of place in the adventure stories which influenced Golding.
    - He is good-looking, charismatic and popular.
    - He is elected democratically and tries to run things fairly.
    - He is practical, building shelters and looking at ways of being rescued.
    - Contrast with Jack – Jack becomes more powerful as Ralph becomes less powerful.
    - Although tempted to join Jack's gang, he resists savagery.
    - At the end he still believes in 'civilization and good behaviour' but has experienced evil and savagery.

14. *Lord of the Flies*
    - Golding's characters are English public schoolboys, representatives of the 'civilized' world.
    - At first they behave as they would expect adults to, electing a leader and making rules.
    - Rivalries, fights etc. are usual in schools but here they get out of hand.
    - The role of Jack and the hunters.
    - The symbolism of the conch and the beast.
    - Changes in the way the boys speak.
    - Stages in the escalation of violence: killing the pig, Piggy, Simon.
    - What happens at the end? Has civilization broken down or have we just learned how superficial the idea is?

15. *Telling Tales*
    - 'The Invisible Mass of the Back Row' starts in Jamaica and moves to England.
    - The narrator describes sights, smells and tastes of the West Indies.
    - In school she is taught a version of history and culture she does not recognize.
    - Moving to England, she feels the difference in cultures but makes friends with girls from similar backgrounds.
    - In England she finds out more about black history and identity, and finds her voice.
    - The narrative is in Standard English but most of the dialogue is in Jamaican dialect.
    - Compare with Carla finding Polish identity in 'My Polish Teacher's Tie'.
    - Compare with the narrator's return to Japan in 'A Family Supper'.
    - Compare with Elizabeth's sense of identity in 'The Odour of Chrysanthemums' or the narrator's in 'Chemistry'.

16. *Telling Tales*
    - Carla introduces herself at the beginning.
    - She tells the story in the past tense, in chronological order.
    - The tone is colloquial, as if she is explaining what happened to someone she knows.
    - She reflects on her own feelings and motives.
    - Through the story she reveals more about her background as it becomes more important to her.
    - She feels different from the teachers / almost invisible to them.
    - Compare with narrator of 'The Invisible Mass of the Back Row' finding her voice but with a different attitude.
    - Compare with 'Chemistry'. Carla is more in control and more perceptive; the boy in 'Chemistry' is an unreliable narrator.

17. *Animal Farm*
    - He is loyal and hard-working, and not intelligent.
    - He does not get involved in ideas and politics.
    - He is exploited by both Mr Jones and the pigs, though he does not see it.

- In terms of the Russian Revolution he represents the non-political working class or 'proletariat'. The revolution was supposed to be for them.
- He is presented as a sympathetic character.
- He is essential for the running of the farm.
- His death shows how little he is valued.

18. *Animal Farm*
- *Animal Farm* as an allegory of the Russian Revolution.
- *Animal Farm* as a fable – not just about one historical event but a moral tale about all revolutions.
- At the start Orwell clearly shows the need for change.
- Major's vision of fairness and equality is inspiring.
- The rebellion has the backing of all and appears to be spontaneous.
- There is a need for leaders, which creates a love of power and corruption.
- Is Orwell saying all revolutions must fail or just describing where they have gone wrong?

Page 53

19. *Never Let Me Go*
- They are called guardians, not teachers. What is the difference?
- In some ways they act like conventional teachers, but some things they do – such as the 'sex lectures' or the gallery – are odd.
- They know about the children's future but only give little bits of information.
- They are part of the system and controlled by the system.
- Miss Geraldine is the most popular guardian and is a stereotype of the popular female teacher.
- Miss Lucy's talks with Tommy show her doubts about the school. She is 'idealistic'.
- Miss Emily's views are ambiguous. She works within society as it is.

20. *Never Let Me Go*
- Madame and her gallery are sources of speculation to the students.
- Most students are keen to get work in the gallery, but are not sure why.
- Tommy thinks the art work is used to decide whether couples can get 'deferrals'.
- The gallery becomes the focus of Tommy and Kathy's hope.
- Kathy, Tommy and Ruth go to a real gallery in Norfolk. It is here that Ruth's hopes of finding her 'model' are dashed.
- The gallery is part of the focus on being 'creative' at Hailsham – an attempt to make the students more human or to prove they are human, perhaps.
- Think about Miss Emily's rather confusing and self-justifying explanation at the end of the novel.

21. *Anita and Me*
- Some of the neighbours' behaviour is casual, even unknowing, racism.
- The dog's name causes Meena to question racist language: 'it's like a swear word'.
- Sam's behaviour at the fete is more openly racist – Meena feels personally hurt.
- Casual racist language used against Meena's mother.
- Racist violence against Aunty Usha is reported and Sam's racism culminates in beating up Mr Bhatra.
- The reference to 'Paki bashing' suggests an acceptance of racism which Meena has not been aware of.
- First-person narrative gives empathy to Meena and the reader shares her growing awareness.
- References to *To Kill A Mockingbird*, and the marked similarity of the ending to that novel's ending.

22. *Anita and Me*
- Mrs Worrall represents the positive side of the Tollington community.
- Her baking fascinates Meena, who is more interested in it than in her mother's cooking.
- She is welcoming and not prejudiced.
- Her family life is seen as sad. She cares for her husband but has no contact with children.
- British families are implicitly criticized in comparison to Indian families.
- Nanima represents the family's Indian roots.
- She cannot speak English and dresses traditionally.
- She shows the importance of the family and reconnects Meena to the family.

23. *Pigeon English*
- Narrator uses dialect expressions such as 'Asweh' and 'hutious'.
- Harri is regularly in touch with his father and sister in Ghana.
- Memories of life in Africa and differences from his present life.
- Importance of the church as centre of the community for Africans.
- Religious/moral principles and traditions.
- Culture of school / the estate.
- Gang culture giving sense of belonging.

24. *Pigeon English*
- Much of the action takes place in school.
- Harri's attitude to school and learning.
- Relationships in school – Dean, the gang, Poppy, the teachers.
- School seems innocent at first, seen through Harri's eyes, with normal activities like playing games and making friends.
- However, we realize it is a dangerous place where bullying and violence are accepted.
- Life in school reflects life on the streets.

Page 54 English Literature Paper 2 – Modern Texts and Poetry. Section B: Poetry

For both questions 25 and 26, look at the mark scheme below, decide which description is closest to your answer and then decide which mark to give yourself up to a maximum of **[30]**.

Marks	Skills
26–30	You have compared texts in an exploratory and critical way. You have used precise, appropriate references to support your interpretation. You have analysed the writer's methods using subject terminology appropriately. You have explored the effects of the writer's methods. You have explored links between text and ideas/context.
21–25	You have made thoughtful, developed comparisons. You have used appropriate references to support your interpretation. You have examined the writer's methods using subject terminology effectively. You have examined the effects of the writer's methods. You have thoughtfully considered links between text and ideas/context.

25. Your answer might include:
- Direct address to the loved one – 'When We Two Parted', 'Love's Philosophy', 'Winter Swans', 'Neutral Tones'.
- Appeal to the loved one – 'Love's Philosophy'.
- Use of sonnet form – compare with other forms used.
- Regular and controlled rhyme and metre – 'When We Two Parted', 'Neutral Tones'.
- Intense love – 'Love's Philosophy', 'Porphyria's Lover'.
- Mutual love – 'Winter Swans'.
- Use of natural imagery – 'Neutral Tones', 'Love's Philosophy', 'Winter Swans', 'The Farmer's Bride'.

26. Your answer might include:
- The poet witnesses the suffering but is not personally involved – contrast 'Remains'.
- Suffering both physical and psychological – 'Remains', 'Exposure'.
- Regularity of form, metre and rhyme – 'The Charge of the Light Brigade', 'Storm on the Island', contrast with other poems.
- Repetition – 'Remains', 'The Charge of the Light Brigade'.
- Suffering caused by the powerful – 'Ozymandias', 'The Charge of the Light Brigade'.
- Suffering of ordinary people – 'The Émigrée', 'Bayonet Charge'.
- Urban setting – 'The Émigrée', 'Remains' – contrast 'The Prelude', 'Storm on the Island'.
- Angry tone – contrast 'Kamikaze', 'Exposure'.

Page 56 English Literature Paper 2 – Modern Texts and Poetry. Section C: Unseen Texts

27.1 Look at the mark scheme below, decide which description is closest to your answer and then decide which mark to give yourself up to a maximum of **[24]**.

Marks	Skills
21–24	You have explored the text critically. You have used precise references to support your interpretation. You have analysed the writer's methods using appropriate subject terminology. You have explored the effects of the writer's methods on the reader.
17–20	You have responded thoughtfully to the text. You have used appropriate references to support your interpretation. You have examined the writer's methods using subject terminology effectively. You have examined the effects of the writer's methods on the reader.

Your answer might include comments on:
- Poem in three regular stanzas.
- Impact of short rhyming couplet in lines 5 and 6 of each stanza.
- It starts with a grand, general statement and then gives examples.
- The third stanza addresses the reader directly.
- Death is a 'leveller' because it is the same for everyone and all are equal.
- Personification of Death ('his icy hand').
- Identification of classes of people by things associated with them ('Sceptre and Crown', 'scythe and spade') – called 'metonymy' in literary criticism.
- The poem reads like a warning.
- The language reflects decay: 'dust', 'wither'.
- There are many words associated with surrender and powerlessness: 'tumble', 'yield', 'stoop', 'captives'.
- For most of the poem the tone is negative – it seems as if no human activity is worthwhile as it all ends in death.
- The last two lines give hope of a kind, an idea that 'the just' can leave something behind.

27.2 Look at the mark scheme below, decide which description is closest to your answer and then decide which mark to give yourself up to a maximum of **[8]**.

Marks	Skills
7–8	You have explored comparisons of the writers' use of language, structure and form, using appropriate subject terminology. You have convincingly compared the effects of the writers' methods on the reader.
5–6	You have thoughtfully compared the writers' use of language and/or structure and/or form, using effective subject terminology. You have clearly compared the effects of the writers' methods on the reader.

Your answer might include comments on:
- The first is about death in general, the second about the death of an individual.
- Stevenson speaks of how he would like to be remembered; Shirley implies no-one will be remembered.
- Stevenson expresses contentment with both life and death. Shirley's view of death is not comforting.
- Both focus on what remains: the grave; the dust.
- Rhythm, rhyme and alliteration give Stevenson's poem a cheerful tone. Shirley's is more ponderous, with a heavy beat.
- Both poets use the second person, 'you', but for Stevenson 'you' seems to be a loved one, while for Shirley it is anyone who reads the poem.

Notes

ACKNOWLEDGEMENTS

The author and publisher are grateful to the copyright holders for permission to use quoted materials and images.

P.30 Extract from 'Walking Away' from THE GATE AND OTHER POEMS by C Day Lewis reprinted by permission of Peters Fraser & Dunlop (www.petersfraserdunlop.com) on behalf of the Estate of C Day Lewis. P.30 'Winter Swans' Copyright © Owen Sheers 2005. Reproduced by permission of the author c/o Rogers, Coleridge & White Ltd., 20 Powis Mews, London W11 1JN. P.30 'Mother, any distance' by Simon Armitage, Copyright © Simon Armitage. P.30 'Checking Out Me History', John Agard, *Alternative Anthem: Selected Poems with Live DVD* (Bloodaxe Books, 2009). P.30 'War Photographer' Copyright © Carol Ann Duffy 1985. Reproduced by permission of the author c/o Rogers, Coleridge & White Ltd., 20 Powis Mews, London W11 1JN. P.30 *Storm on the Island* from 'Death of a Naturalist' by Seamus Heaney (Faber and Faber Ltd).

All images are © Shutterstock.com

Every effort has been made to trace copyright holders and obtain their permission for the use of copyright material. The author and publisher will gladly receive information enabling them to rectify any error or omission in subsequent editions. All facts are correct at time of going to press.

Published by Collins
An imprint of HarperCollins*Publishers*
1 London Bridge Street
London SE1 9GF

© HarperCollins*Publishers* Limited 2020

ISBN 9780008326715

Content first published 2015
This edition published 2020

10 9 8 7 6 5 4 3 2

All rights reserved. No part of this publication may be reproduced, stored in a retrieval system, or transmitted, in any form or by any means, electronic, mechanical, photocopying, recording or otherwise, without the prior permission of Collins.

British Library Cataloguing in Publication Data.

A CIP record of this book is available from the British Library.

Publishing Manager: Rebecca Skinner and Emily Linnett
Commissioning Editor: Katie Galloway
Author: Paul Burns
Editorial: Susan Milligan
Cover Design: Sarah Duxbury and Kevin Robbins
Inside Concept Design: Sarah Duxbury and Paul Oates
Text Design and Layout: Jouve India Private limited
Printed and bound by CPI Group (UK) Ltd, Croydon, CR0 4YY